Steve Adams

Easy Woodturning Projects

Woodturning templates for utensils

Printed and published by: BoD - Books on Demand, Norderstedt
Drawings, illustrations: Steve Adams

2021

ISBN: 9783755716303

Foreword

Woodturning - An old craft is becoming more and more popular

It all started with an elastic long piece of wood. A belt attached to it to turn the workpiece clamped between two centers, the other end attached to a seesaw-like foot switch. Finished was the seesaw lathe, which still finds enthusiastic followers today. Not least because of the low speeds and forces involved, a seesaw lathe is often a first lathe for children, who can thus learn woodturning in a fairly harmless way. It allows you to try out chisels and scraper and learn which tool angle allows you to cut the wood effectively.

In the past a pole lathe was used to produce everyday items right in the forest. The lathe was assembled and disassembled on the spot and the waste wood from the still fresh and green logs remained on the forest floor. It is hard to imagine woodturning in a more ecological way than that. These first woodturners cut the wood with axes and hatchets and turned it into chair legs, struts, and other needed utensils. Furniture from that time that survived to this day bears witness to the accomplished skills of these craftsmen, who still were turning their piece of wood by power of their own muscles.

It was not until the industrial revolution that heavy cast-iron lathes emerged along many machines for metalworking, mainly used by wainwrights, the furniture industry and other wood industries. Special lathes were developed for many applications. For example, the wheelwright's lathe had devices for dividing and drilling wheel hubs and rims, and picture frames were turned on face lathes even before the invention of milling machines. These lathes were usually driven by leather belts placed on smaller or larger drive pulleys depending on the desired speed. This way, different speeds became possible using steam or water power engines. In addition, woodturners could now turn their workpieces in one session, as it rotated continuously. With the invention and inexpensive production of electric motors, the lathe became independent of the central power source used for the whole workshop. This made it interesting and affordable even for hobbyists.

However, the craft of woodturning did not stop at this stage of development. Electronics, computers, pneumatic equipment and new steel types for tools became available and allowed an enormous increase in production speeds. Finally, these semi-automatic and fully automatic machines heralded the end of hand turning. The classic craft of woodturning was and still is in danger of dying out. Curtain rods, dresser knobs, children's toys - once made in the woodturner's workshop, are now produced in automatic lathe shops in a matter of seconds.

An ever-growing community of recreational turners is trying to counter this trend. They partly use old machines that nowadays still can be found very cheap on second-hand markets. With great attention to detail, enthusiasts restore cast-iron lathes and equip them with electric motors if still belt-driven. They not only love woodturning but also value old mechanical engineering, which in some aspects is superior to today's amateur lathes. The main difference to today's constructions (with a few exceptions) is the bed and the feet. In the past, these were mostly made of heavy cast-iron. This weight resulted in less vibration. Today, many manufacturers make do with sheet metal and tubular steel constructions. Using such a lathe, as it can be found in various DIY stores, an enthusiastic woodturner will quickly lose interest.

I therefore advise every interested layman to first attend a woodturning course before getting down to business with the advice of a "master" and the woodturning friends he/she has made. For what applies to the quality of a woodturning lathe applies equally to the choice of tools on which one could spend even more money. No matter how great the urge to set up a woodturning workshop as quickly as possible, I advise against it! A woodturning course at the beginning will save you money. Because only here can aspiring woodturners learn what tools they really need.

Today there are companies that specialise in the production of quality lathes and tools. Quality has its price. A good new lathe can quickly exceed thousands euros. If you add accessories, you are easily approaching the price of a small car. However, if you have been bitten by the woodturning bug, you will not shy away from the price and rave about the smoothness and power of your purchase.

This book is not intended to teach the basics of woodturning. It does not intend to be a manual for the correct use of lathes. Rather, it tries to recall objects of everyday use that have perhaps been forgotten in modern days. The fact that these often shapely and practical objects still have their function is proven, for example, by beautiful door wedges, rolling pins, wooden mallets, etc. They all have one thing in common: they work beautifully and are ergonomically shaped. The more we like to touch an object, the longer it can be found in our household. Nowadays, these wooden objects often are replaced by plastic resulting in a limited lifespan as a standard. How delightful it is when an old chisel finds its way into your hands at a garage sale, its handle polished by touch and its frayed end telling of heavy use. That is exactly the feeling this book wants to convey - to recall and revive forgotten utensils!

Wedge

A door wedge is made from tough wood, e.g. ash or robinia. Two wedges can be made at the same time on the lathe. If the wedge is used with the saw face downwards, the knob lifts off the ground and can be conveniently gripped by hand.

A scantling is clamped between the centers. Handles are turned on both sides. The middle part remains square.
When the turning is finished, the scantling is cut diagonally into two wedges by saw.

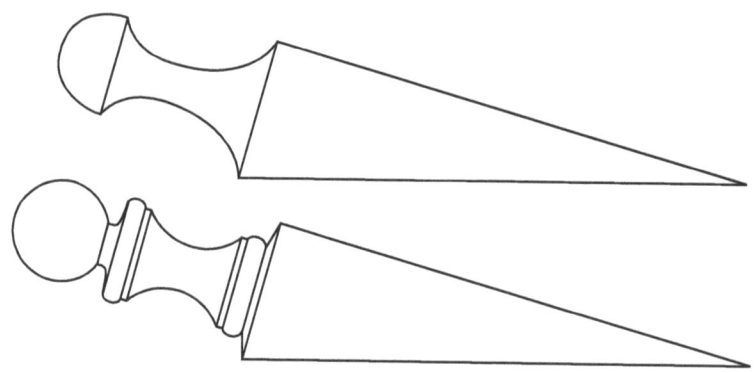

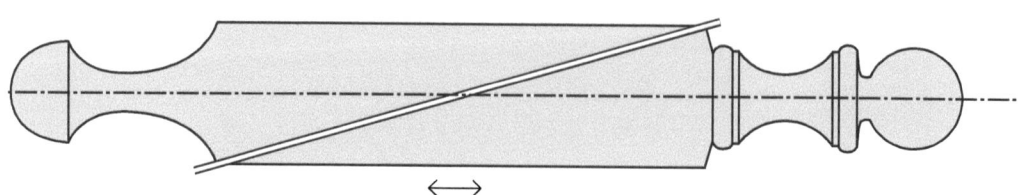

Mallet

Ash is suitable for the head, ash or another tough wood for the handle. If it is a light mallet, the head can also be made of other hardwoods or be glued together from several pieces of wood. The handle is sawn and wedged at the top. The head of the mallet is slightly conical so that more weight lies at the end of the tool. In addition, the cone shape improves the impact effect when clubbing from the wrist.

If the mallet is worn, it can be over-turned. This way it can still be used for light work at the end of its lifespan.

The handle of the mallet is shaped into a knob at the end to prevent slipping.

The usual dimensions and weights of a mallet range from approx. 120 mm diameter with a weight of approx. 1 kg to approx. 180 mm with a weight of approx. 2 kg.

The scantling of the head is bored through and then turned on the outside.

The handle is created as normal spindle turning.

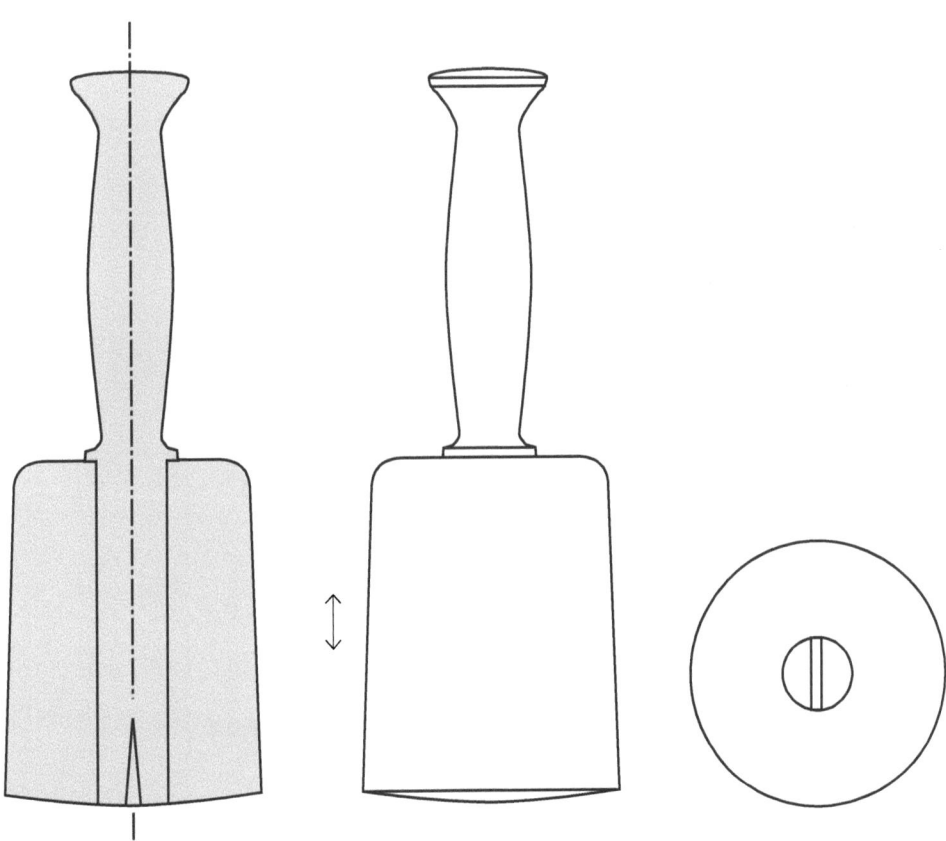

Hammer

Ash is suitable for the head and ash for the handle. The length of the handle and the size and weight of the head are adapted to the respective application. The handle is sawn at the top and wedged at right angles to the grain of the head. If the hammer is intended for heavy use, the ends are fitted with iron rings to prevent the wood from splintering.

The iron rings can either be fitted hot, which then tighten around the wood as they cool down, or they can be made to fit precisely. They are then secured with nails or screws.

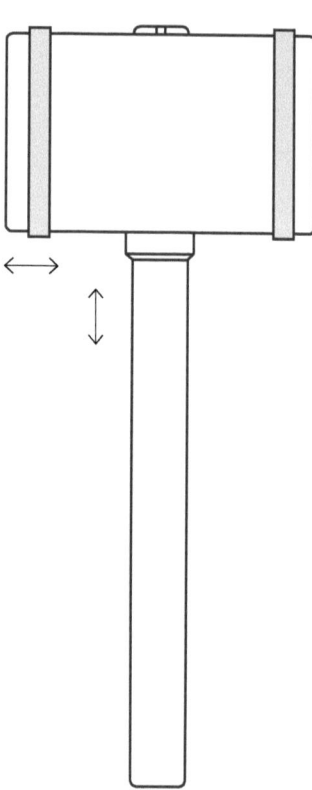

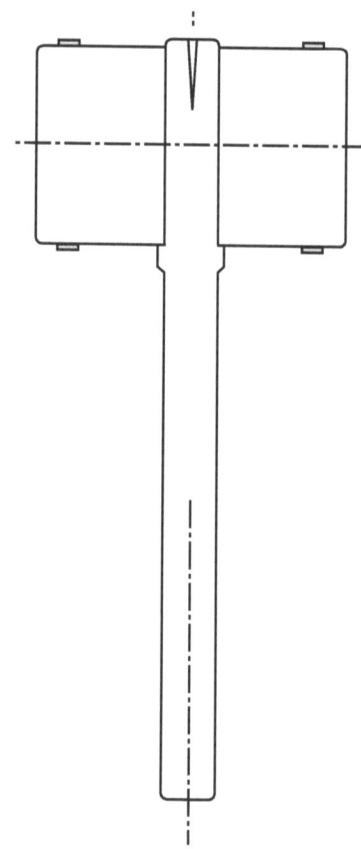

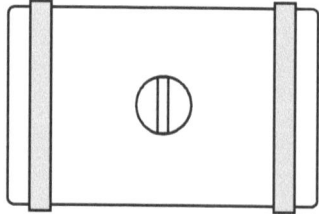

The second version shows a version where the handle is made wider at the top to prevent the head from slipping off. The head is put over the handle and clamped by hitting the top on a wooden stick.

The style and head are normal spindle woodwork and turned between the centers. The hole is drilled to a suitable diameter.

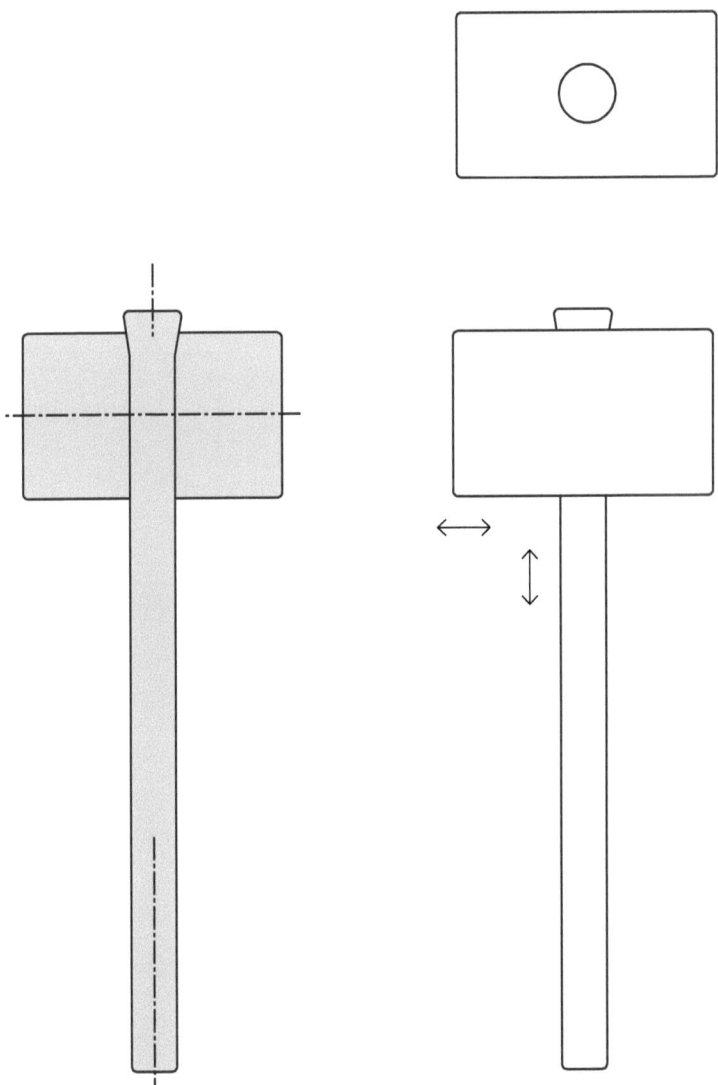

Stakes with cord

The stakes are turned as classic spindle woodwork between the centres. The end of the cord is either held by a small hole using a dowel or simply tied down. A small nail with a round head can also be used.

The stakes for the garden cord have a narrow tip that easily penetrates the soil and a practical handle that should sit good in the hands. In the depression the cord is wound up after use like with a cotton reel.

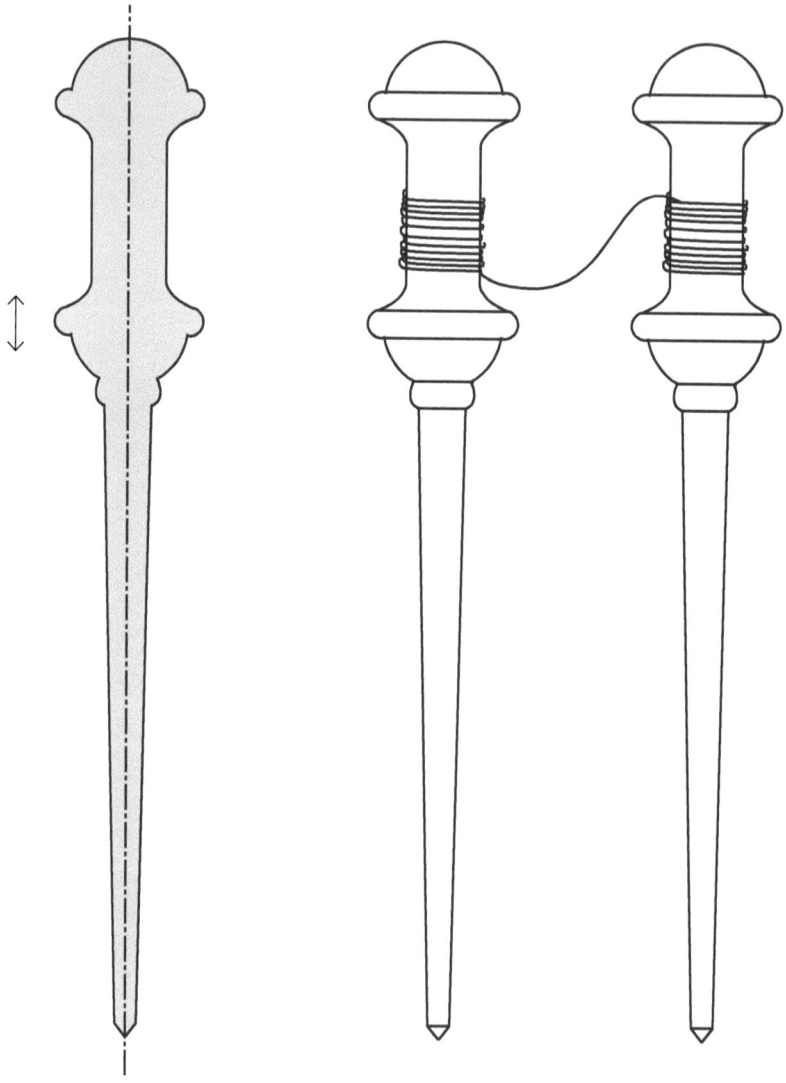

Dibber

One of the oldest garden tools is the dibber. It has an ergonomic handle and a conical tip. This prevents soil from falling back into the hole. Grooves e.g. at intervals of 2.5 or 3 cm enable planting at the same depth.

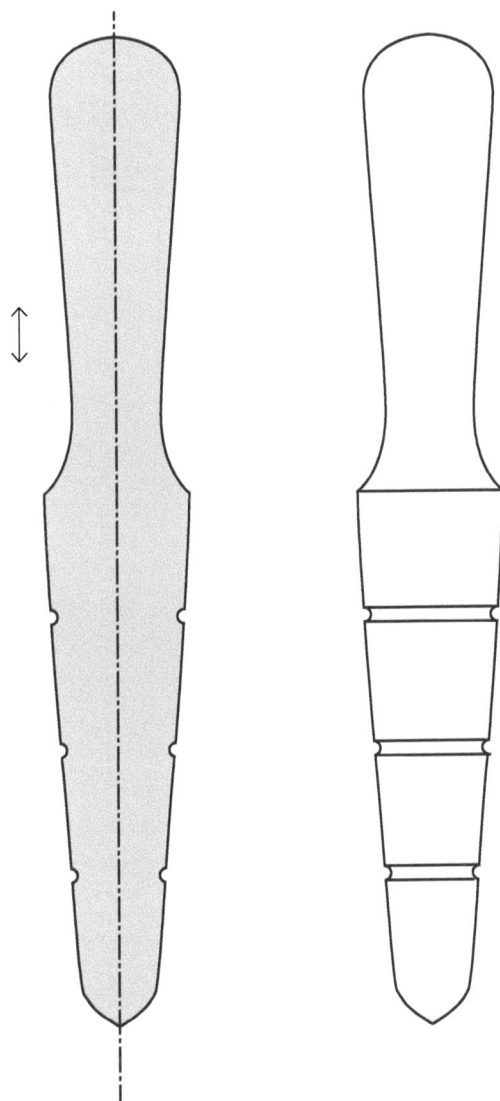

Candlestand

It is still the epitome of festive occasions. It has a solid base and a flat, large ground surface that prevents it from toppling over. A hole of the desired size is drilled in the top, which is fitted with a candle sleeve made form metal. This spout protects the wood if the candle burns down completely and ensures that no accidents will occur.

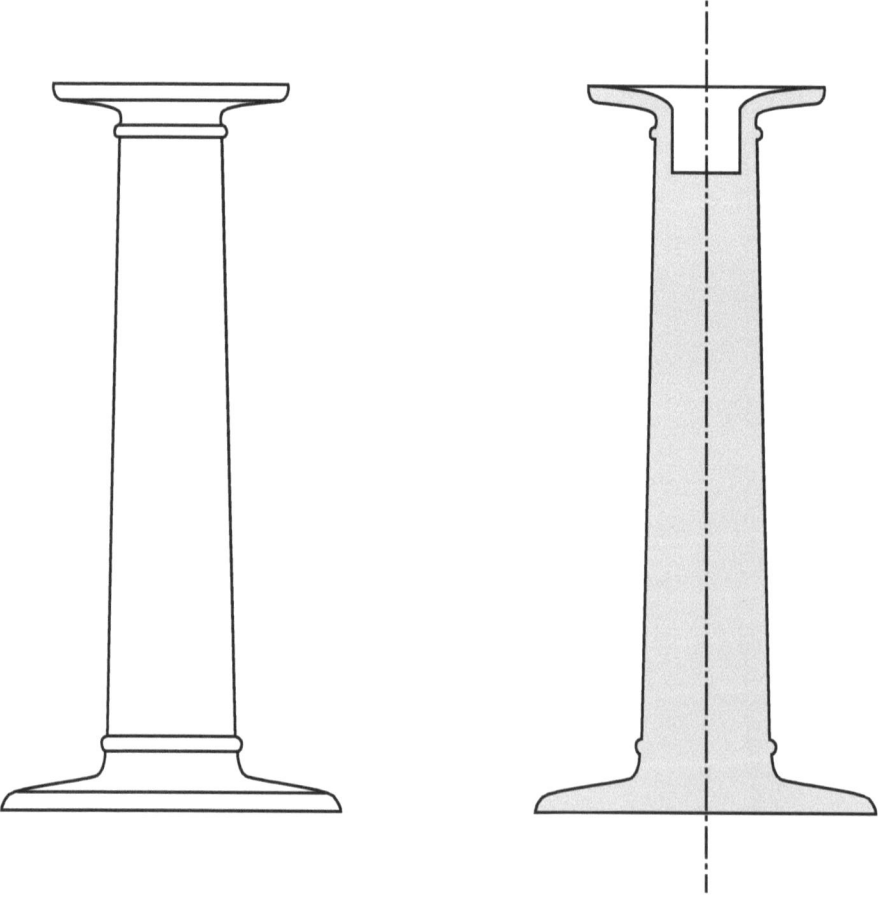

In the past, it was used to see in the dark when walk-
ing through the hallway after dark. Its large bottom
surface protects the floor and tablecloth from wax
stains. It can easily be made of two parts. One as spindle work between the centers, the other as faceplate
work like a bowl.

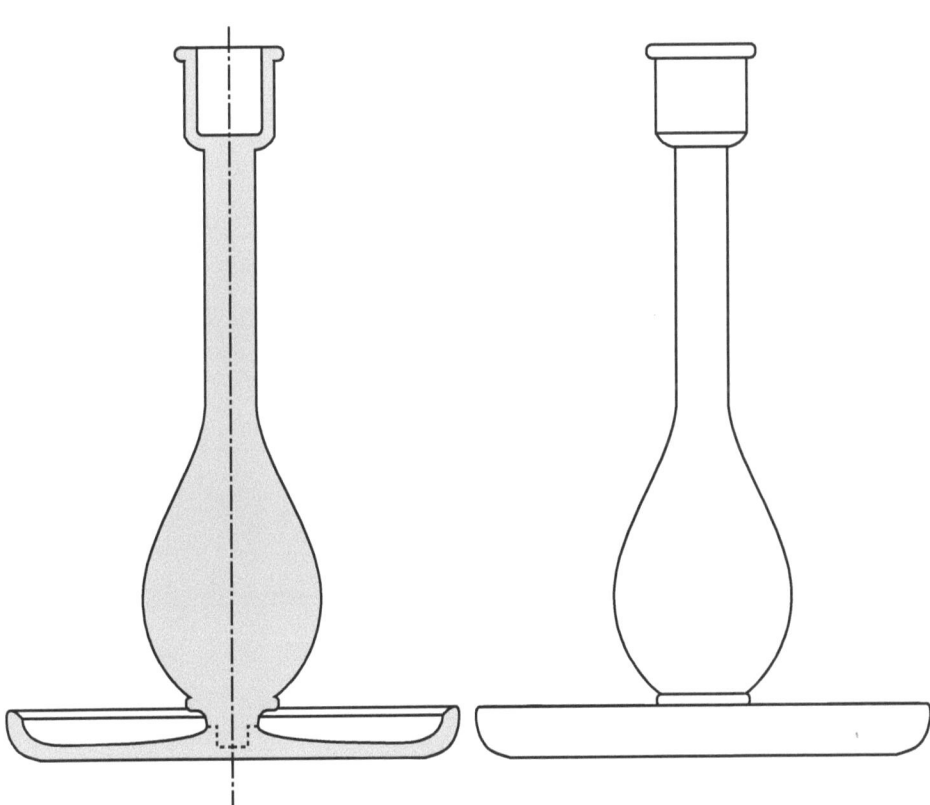

Tealight

Today we encounter tealight holders in a variety of designs and materials. For the woodturner, they are an attractive task, especially to process leftovers. Rare flamed woods make such a tealight holder a jewel on every table. The size of the depression must correspond to the respective tealight inlet. For fire safety reasons, an inlet made of glass is recommended, which then gets filled with a conventional tealight.

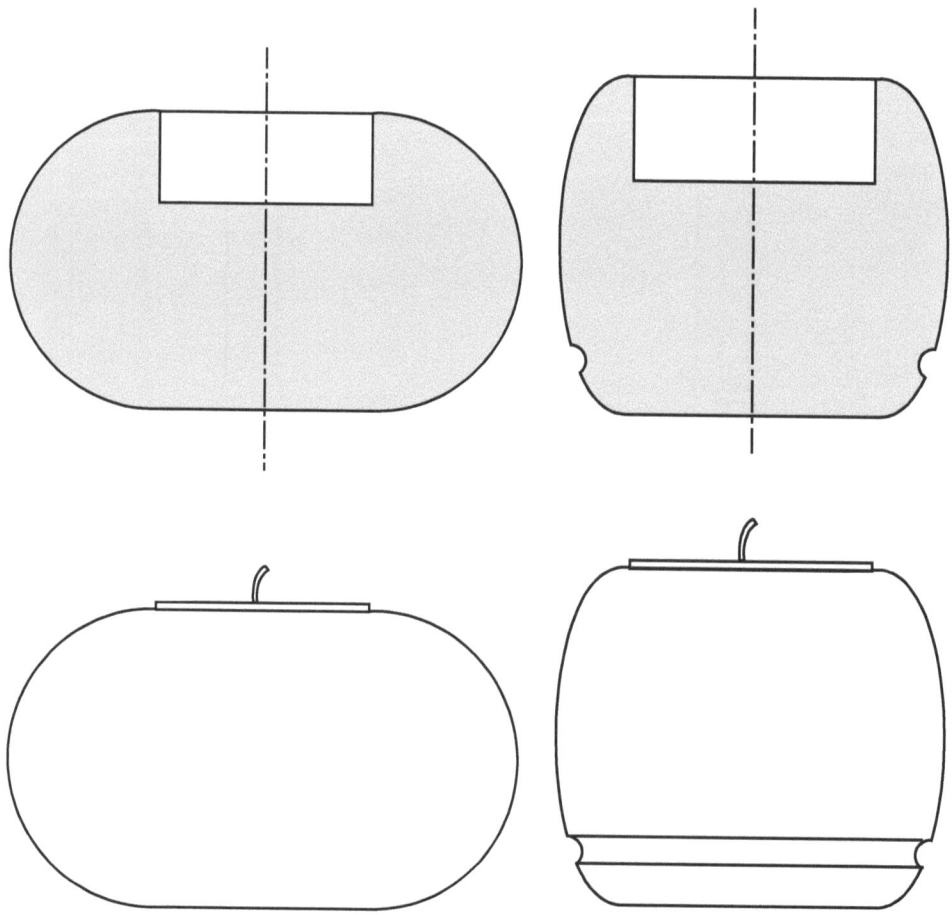

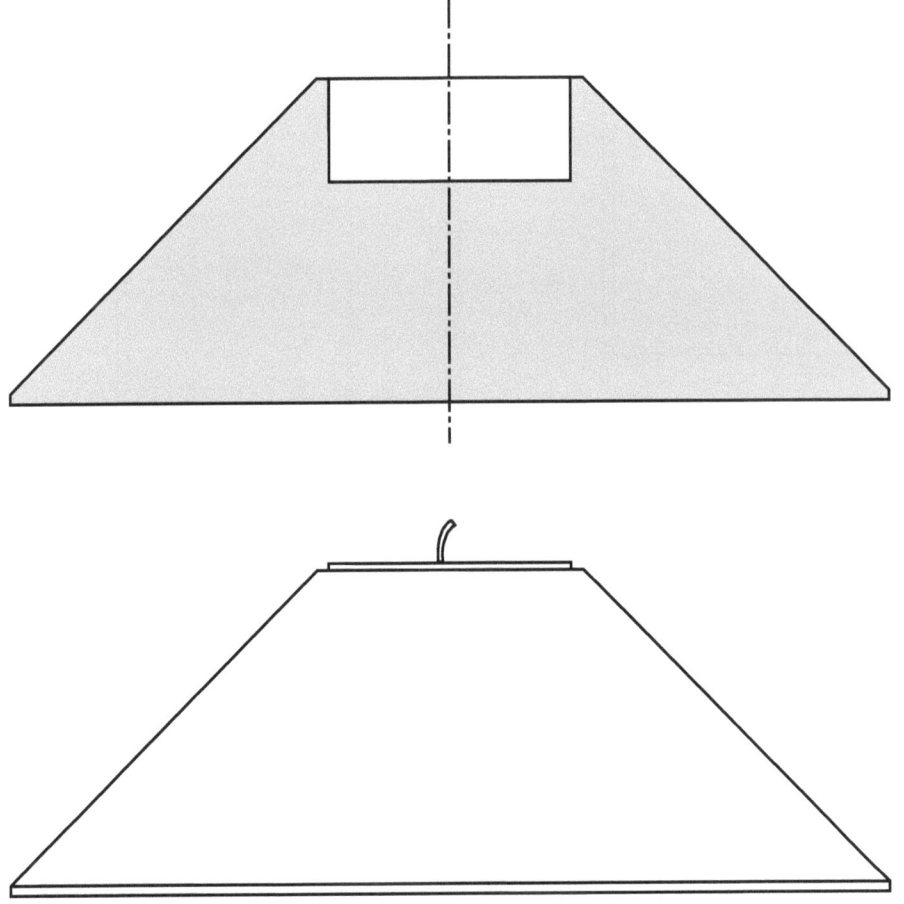

Windlight

A windlight has a bell jar that protects the flame.
However, it is important to ensure that the flame still
gets sufficient oxygen, otherwise the flame will hardly
burn. Here, the problem was solved by drilling holes
into the glass cylinder.

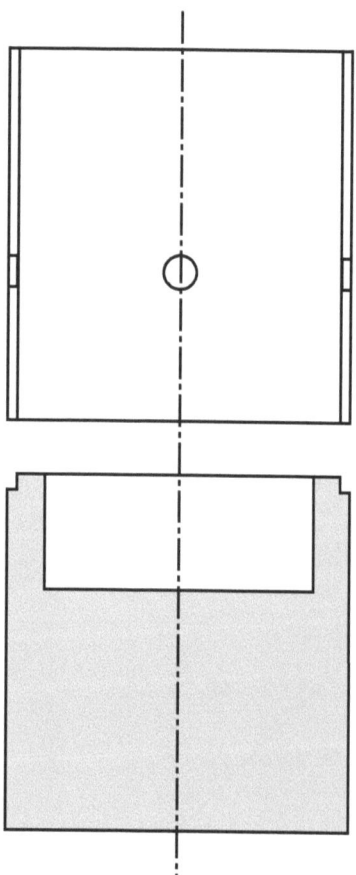

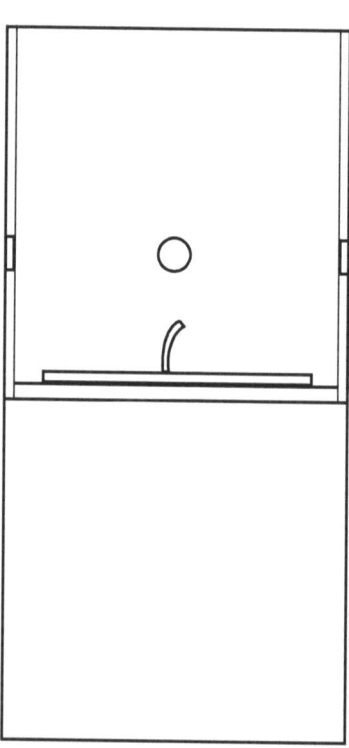

Kite reel

Building and flying a kite has always been a childhood dream for many. A good spindle accommodates the line between two wooden discs. If the spindle is held loosely on both sides, line can be released in a controlled and quick manner. As shown here, the spindle can be made from one piece, or from a rod with dowels for the middle section. Then the handles are glued into pre-drilled holes on each side.

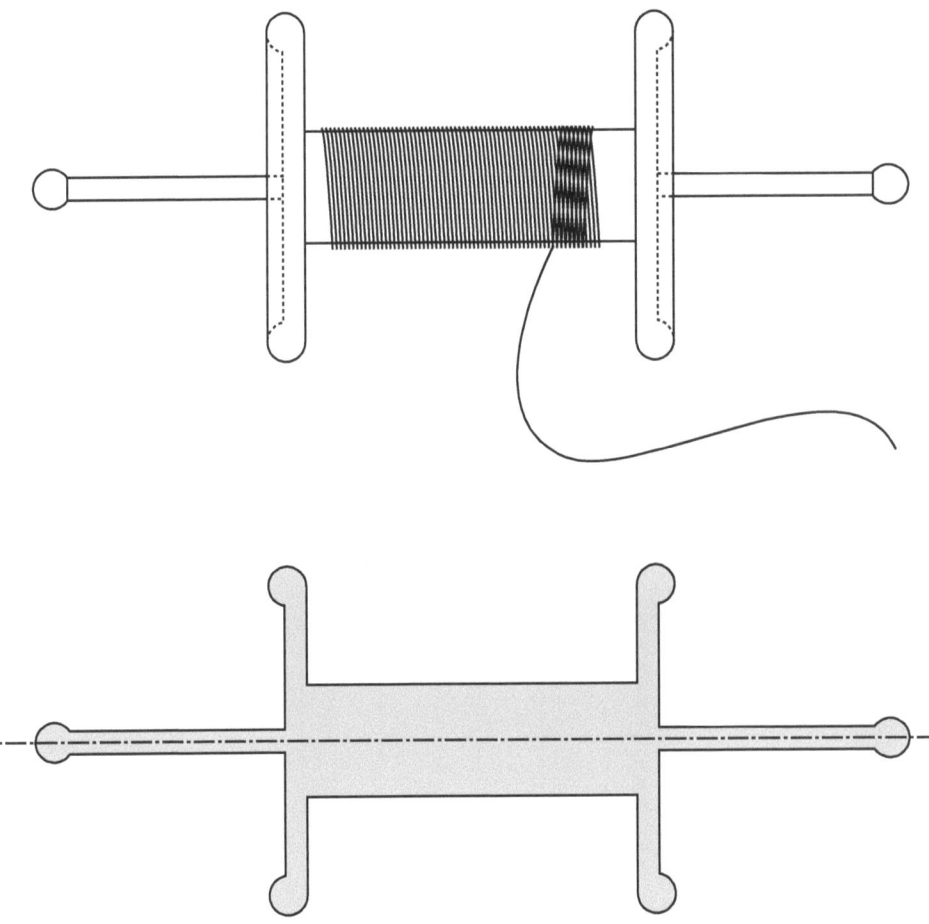

Clothespeg

The classic clothespeg has been almost completely replaced by its plastic version. Wood used for making clothespegs is fine-grained wood such as beech. It is turned as spindle woodwork and then shaped with a saw. The inside of the saws edges are finely sanded before use. Do not use oil, as this could bleed through to the laundry.

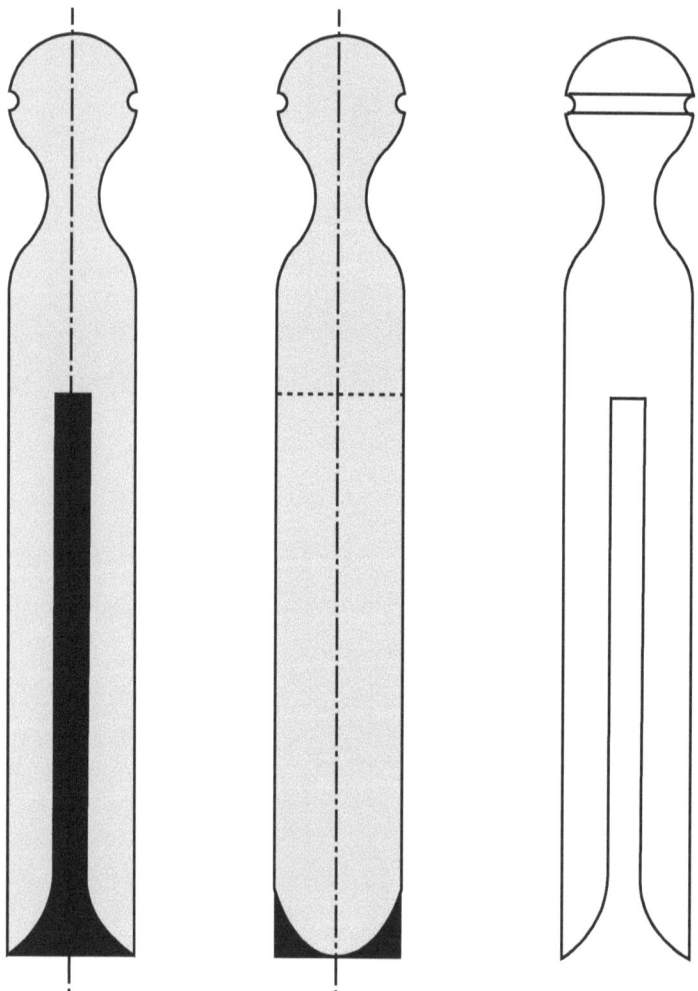

Tray

The classic tray has a large base and a stable edge that prevents placed glasses from sliding down. Many shapes are possible of which some are listed here.

It can be pre-turned from wet wood and turned flat after drying. Or it can be made from a dried thick board.

Potato masher

The ideal tool for preparing mashed potatoes and
other thick mash. Since it comes into direct contact
with food, it should be made of beech, which then can
be rubbed with walnut oil for protection.

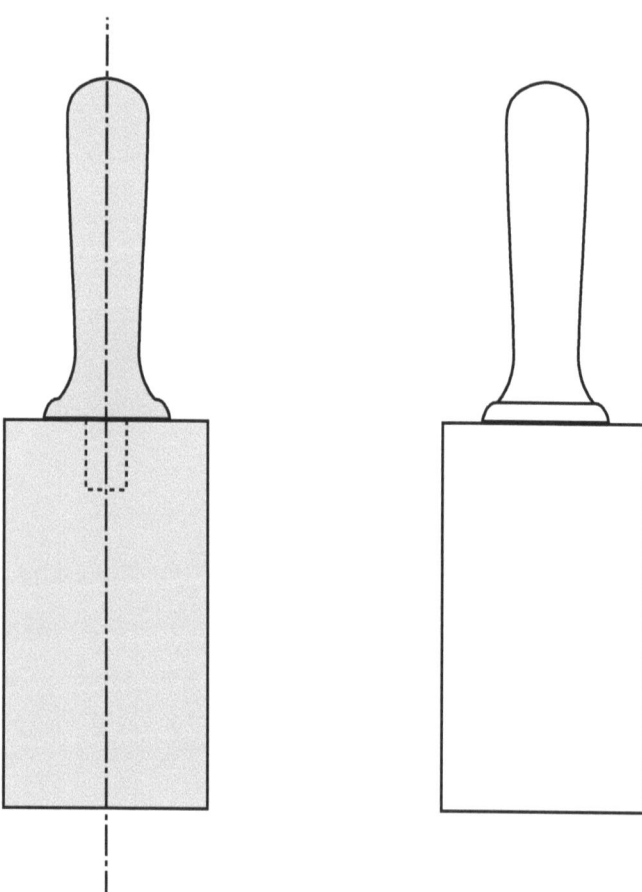

Mushroom masher

If you are dealing with soft-boiled food that needs to be pressed through a sieve, use a mushroom masher. It has a rounded pressure surface which protects the sieve.

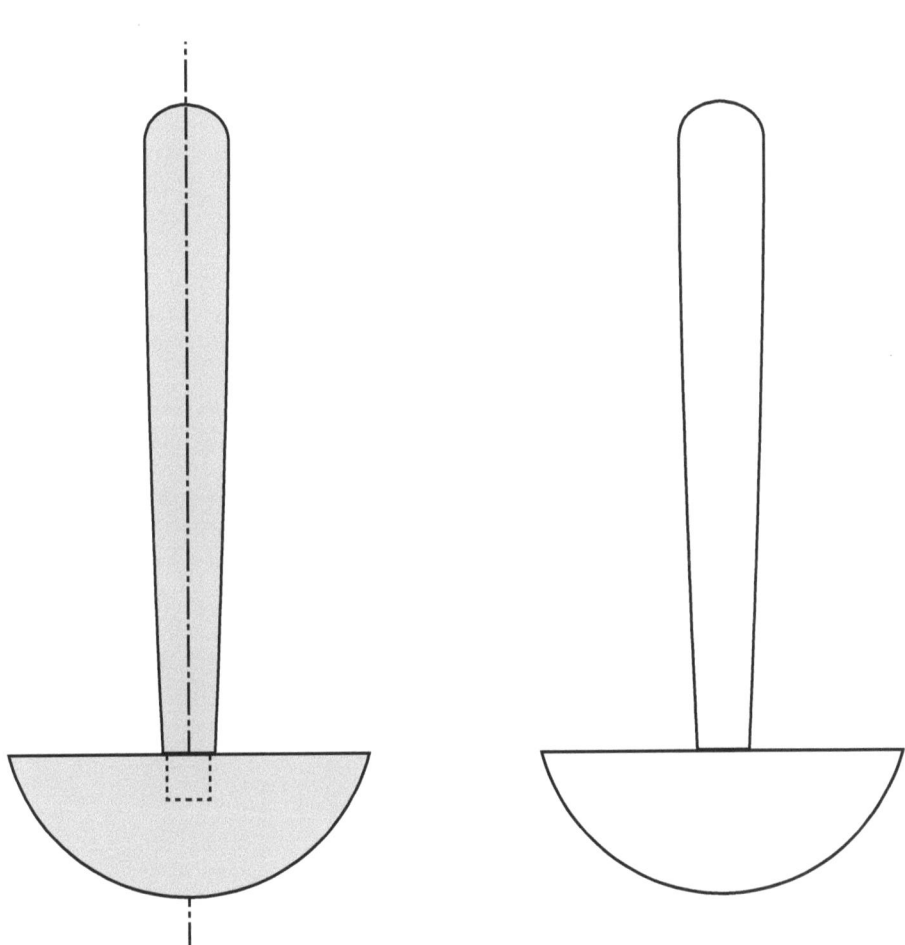

Croquet

A garden game for all ages. The wooden ball is driven through a number of hoops by mallet. The hoops are either made of bent U-shaped wire or with two stakes. This way the ball has to move from the colour-marked target to the peg and back.

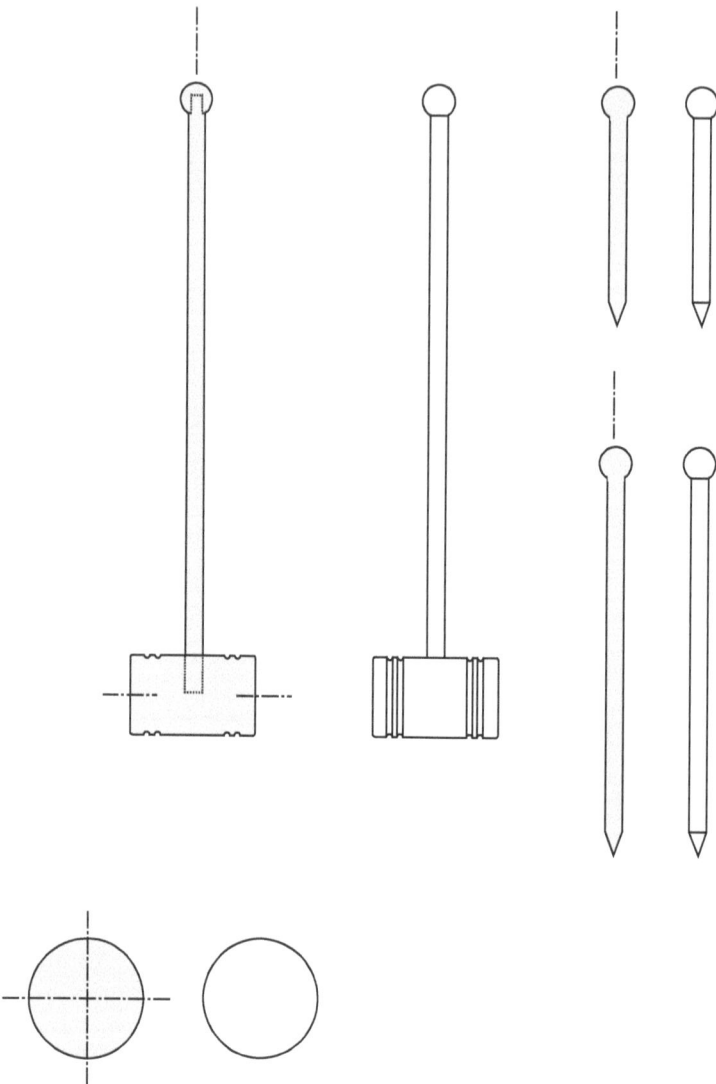

Ninepin

The ninepins should have a small base and quite a lot of weight in the upper part. Only then will they fall properly making it fun to play. Hardwood is preferable for the ninepins and balls.

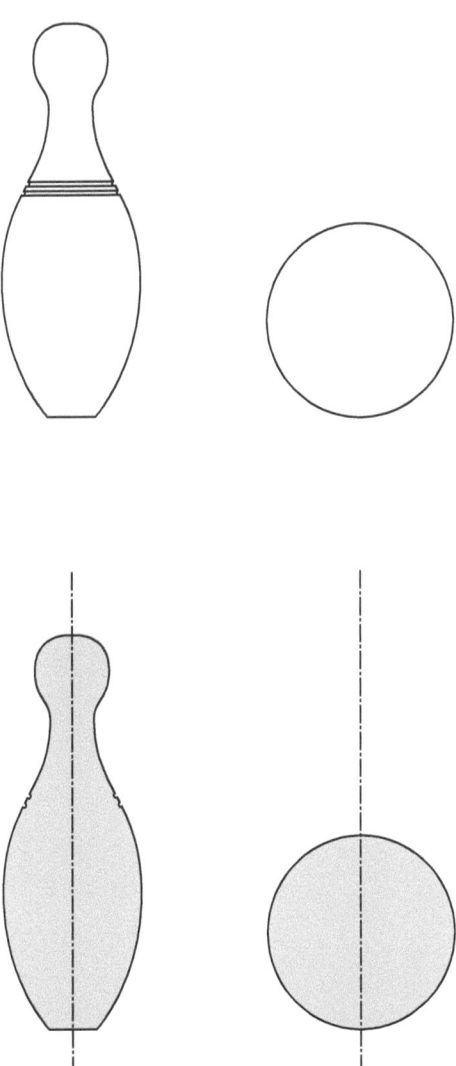

Pyramid game

The pyramid has a curved base that makes it wobble.
Different sized discs can be put on by the toddler. All
edges are rounded to prevent injuries.

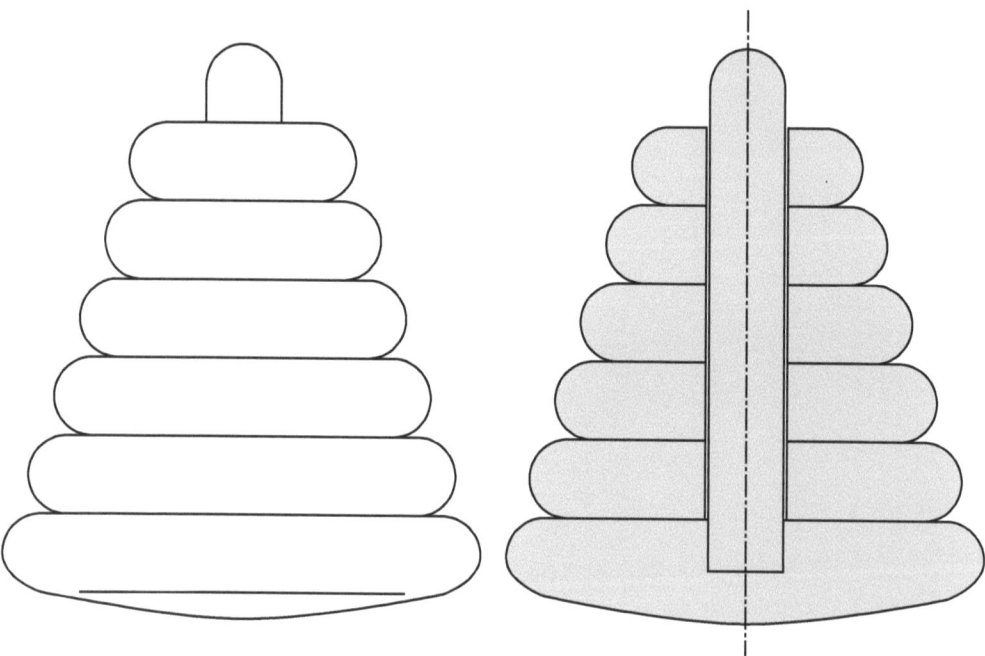

Wobble board

The wobble board promotes a sense of balance. A
multi-layer board is recommended as the material
for the board. The hemisphere is turned like the outer
shape of a bowl. Both parts then are screwed together.

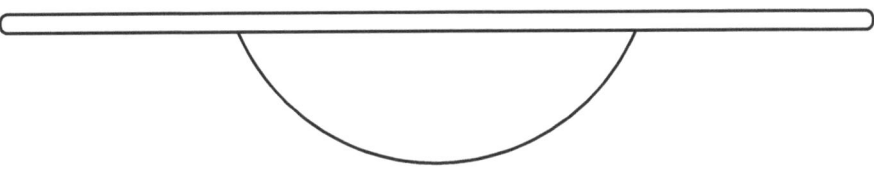

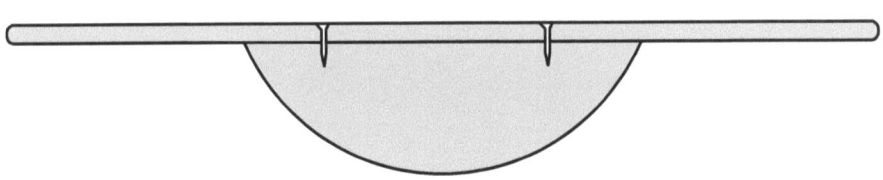

Darning egg

In our throwaway society, the darning egg has become
nothing more than a worry stone. To bring it back to
the collective consciousness, here are two solutions:
one is massiv, the other designed as a caddy. Thread
and needles can be conveniently stored inside.

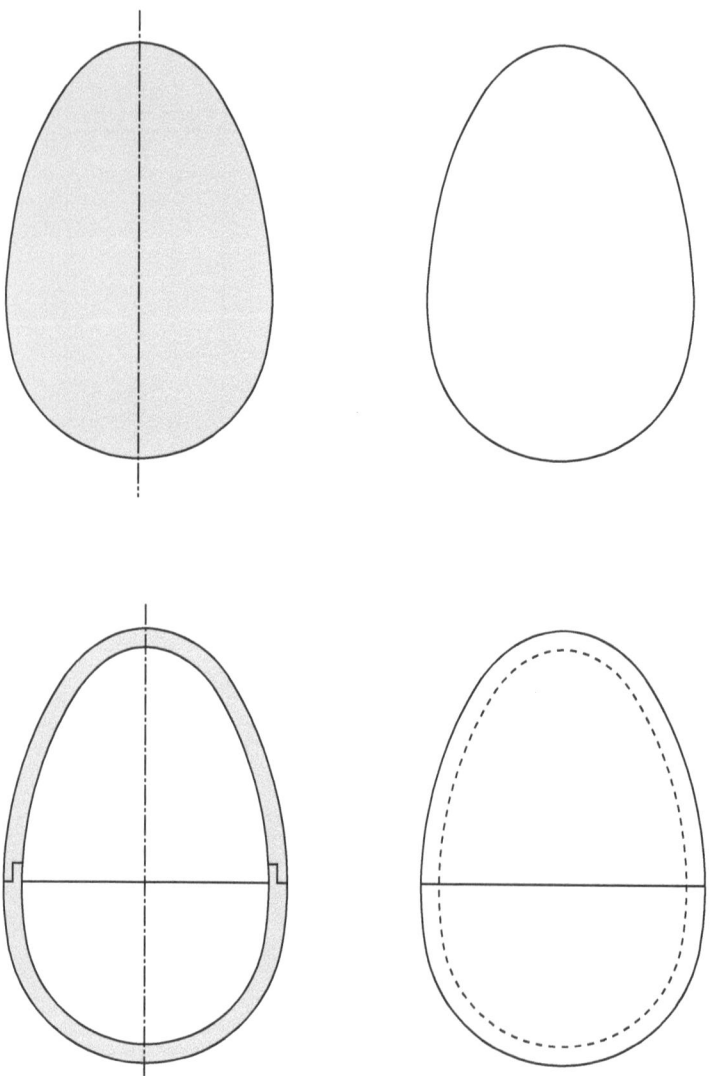

Thimble

With this thimble, there is no need to worry about a chrome or nickel allergy. It is adapted to fit the finger, slips off to a lesser extent than the metal version and is very comfortable to wear.

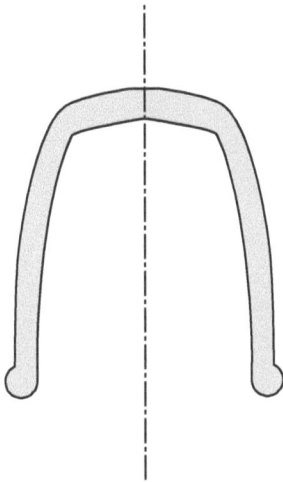

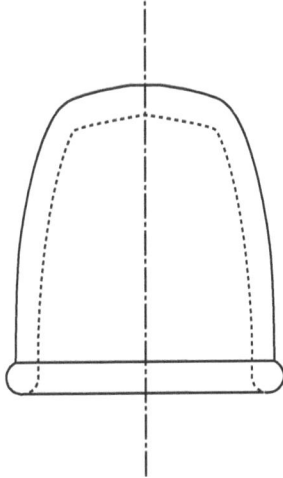

Buttons

Hardwoods whose fibres are very fine can be used for wooden buttons. They may be polished so smooth that they will not pull threads from the fabric.

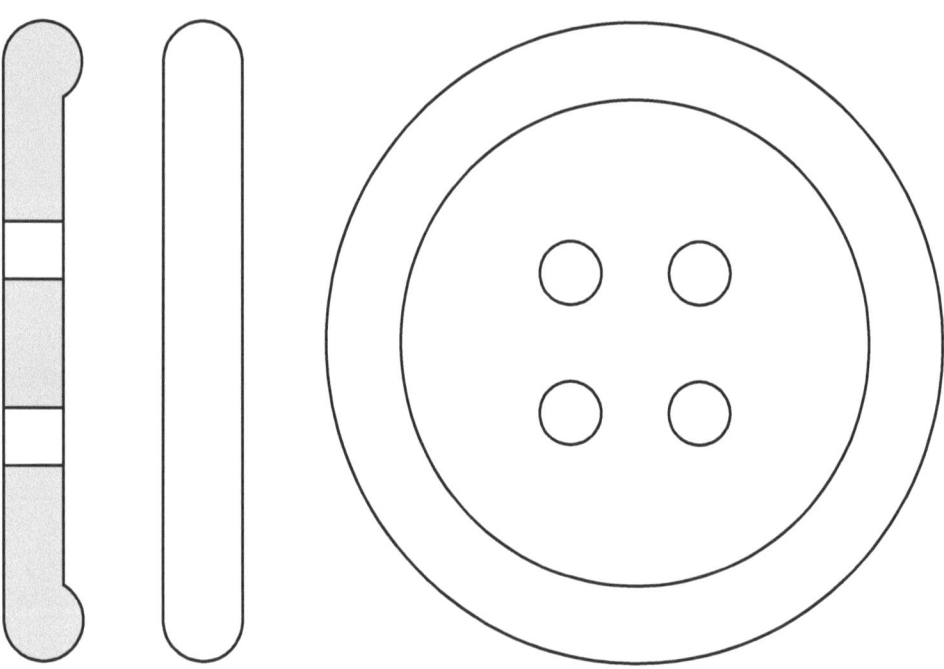

Pepper and salt shaker

They can also be made from high-quality wood. If you use a light and a dark wood, you do not need to label them. The hole in the salt shaker should be approx. 2.5 - 3.5 mm for the salt to trickle out of the shaker. For the pepper shaker, the holes can be made smaller. A rubber stopper at the bottom serves as a seal.

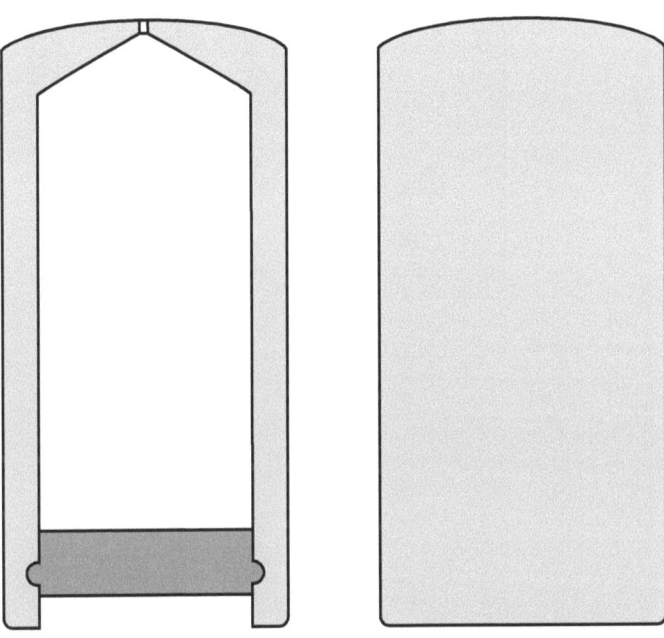

Egg cup

The breakfast egg is not simply eaten from the table. It
can be presented in a filigree goblet or stand upright
in a rustic column. An egg cup should be lacquered or
at least well oiled to protect the wood.

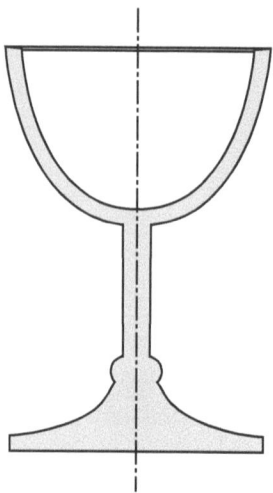

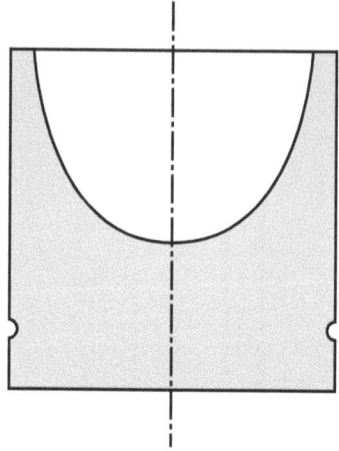

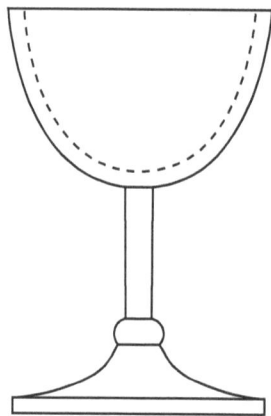

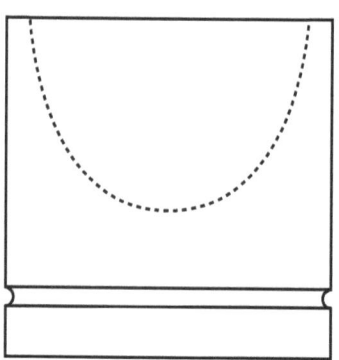

Chopping board

The classic chopping board and bread board is made of wood and still more hygienic than its modern plastic version. It can be fitted with a groove to catch any spilling juices. Beech, ash and other non-toxic hard- woods are suitable. To prevent the board from warping, it can also be glued together from narrow slats.

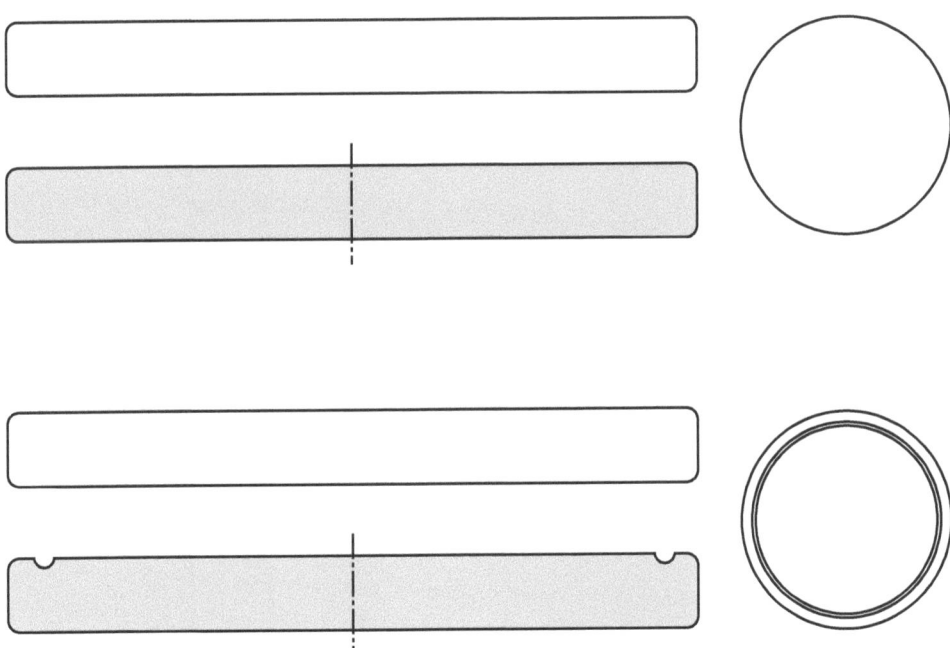

Mezzaluna chopping board

The mezzaluna chopping board is the counterpart to
the mezzaluna knive. Its curved shape keeps the herbs
together when chopping. Hardwood is a good choice
for this board.

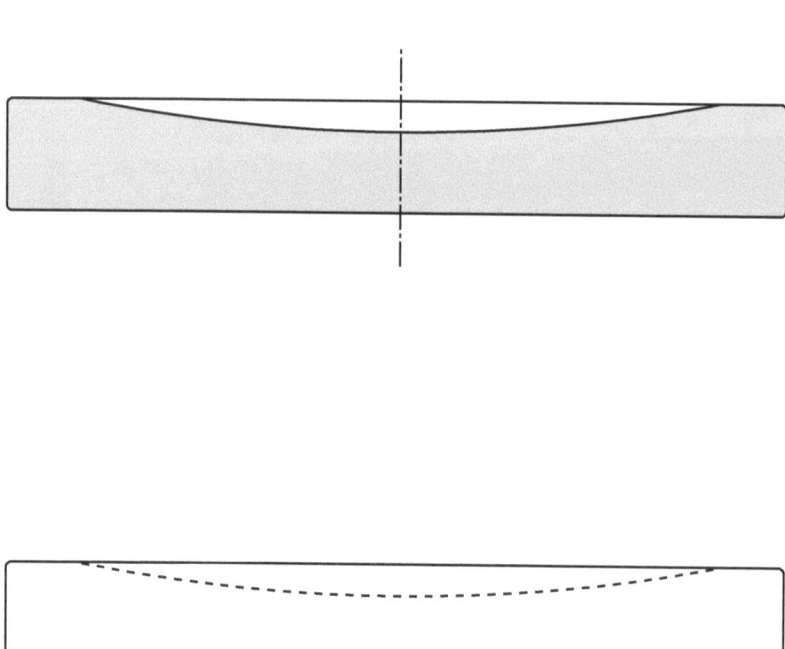

Handles

People like to touch good handles. Depending on the application, they are fitted with metal ferrules (rings) to prevent the wood from splintering.

Handles for chisels and sculpting tools also have a ferrule at the rear end to prevent the wood from splintering due to the hammer blows.

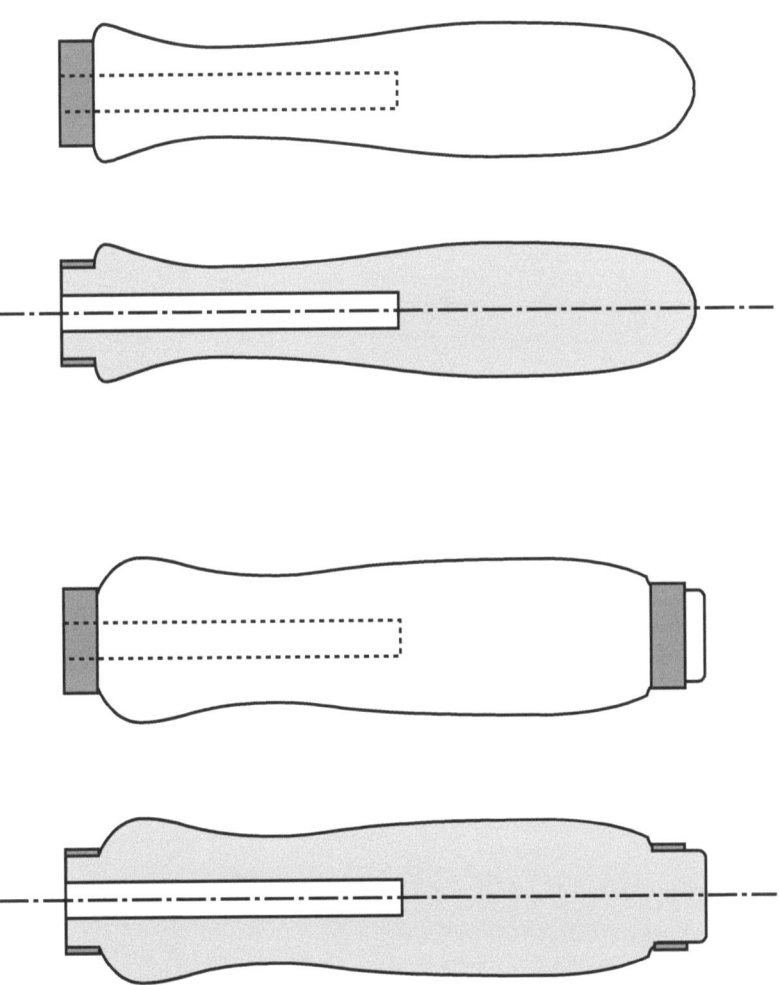

Mortar

A mortar should be made of very hard wood. It is made like a small bowl. The pestle is turned as spindle woodwork.

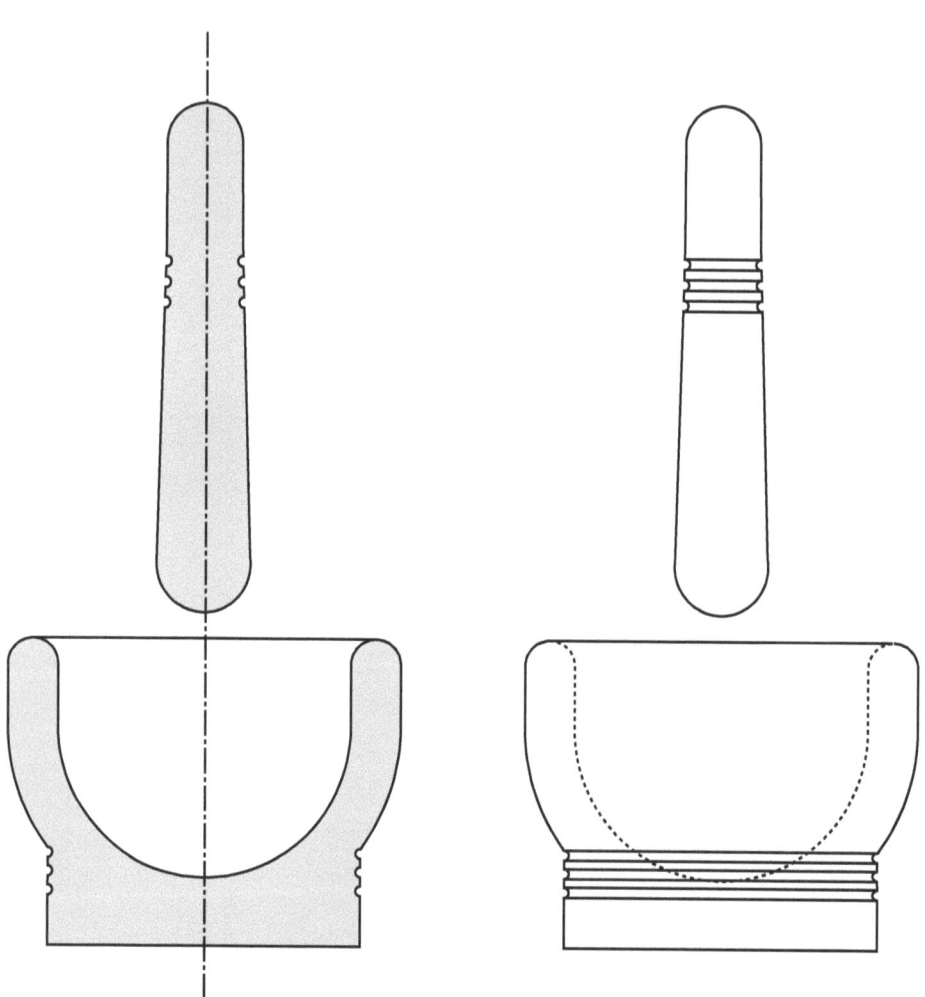

Espresso tamper / Stamp

The espresso tamper is indispensable for manual espresso machines. In the noble version, a turned plate made of aluminium or brass is attached at the bottom. The turned handle is screwed or glued on with a threaded pin. As a utilitarian object, however, it can also be more simply turned from one piece.

Stamps can be made in the same way. Stamp plates, which can be ordered online for little money, are glued onto the flat surface.

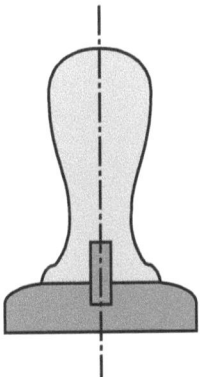
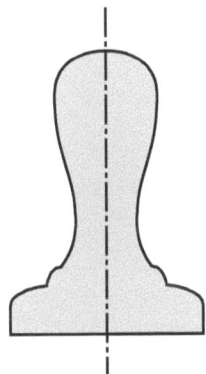
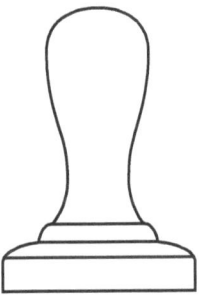

Rolling pin / Dough roller

The classic rolling pin consists of a rod that is rounded on both ends. It is pressed onto the dough with the palms of the hands and rolled.

With the second variant, the mass of the rolling pin helps to do the work. The third version is perforated and equipped with a rotating axle. This makes rolling dough even easier.

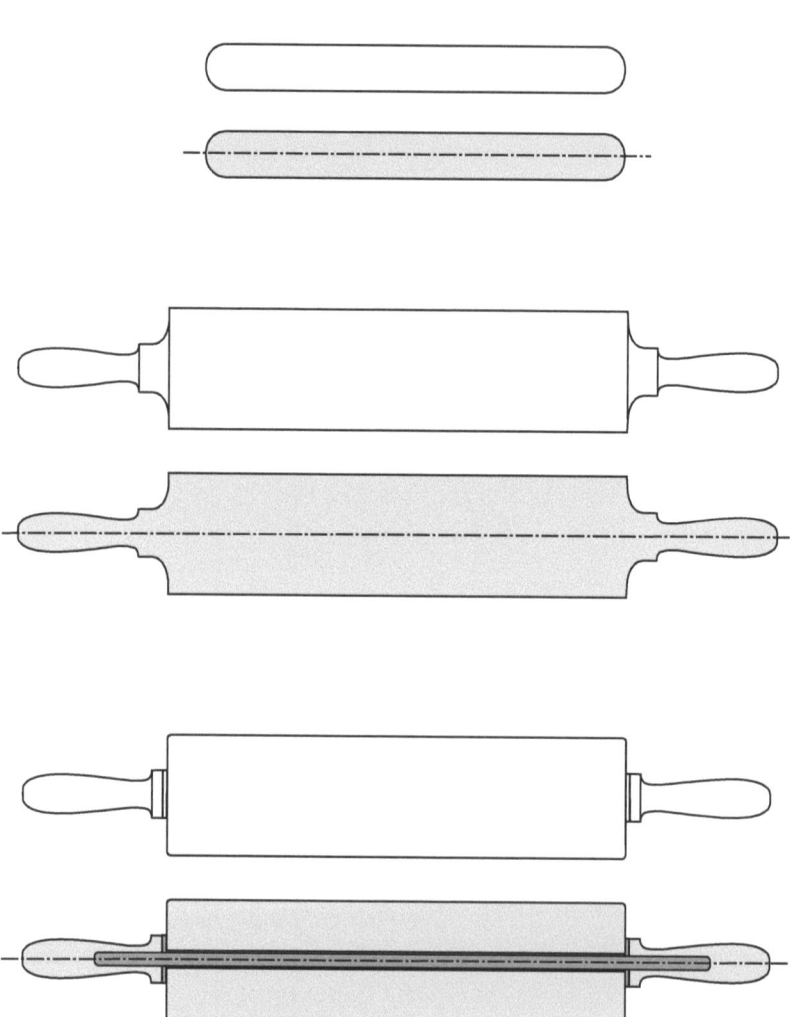

This dough roller is used in the tough business of baking, but created quite easily.

A hole is drilled through handles and roller. A threaded rod is used as the axle. Encapsulated ball bearings at each end ensure excellent running. The handles are secured with nuts on the ball bearing and cap nuts on the ends by locking the nuts.

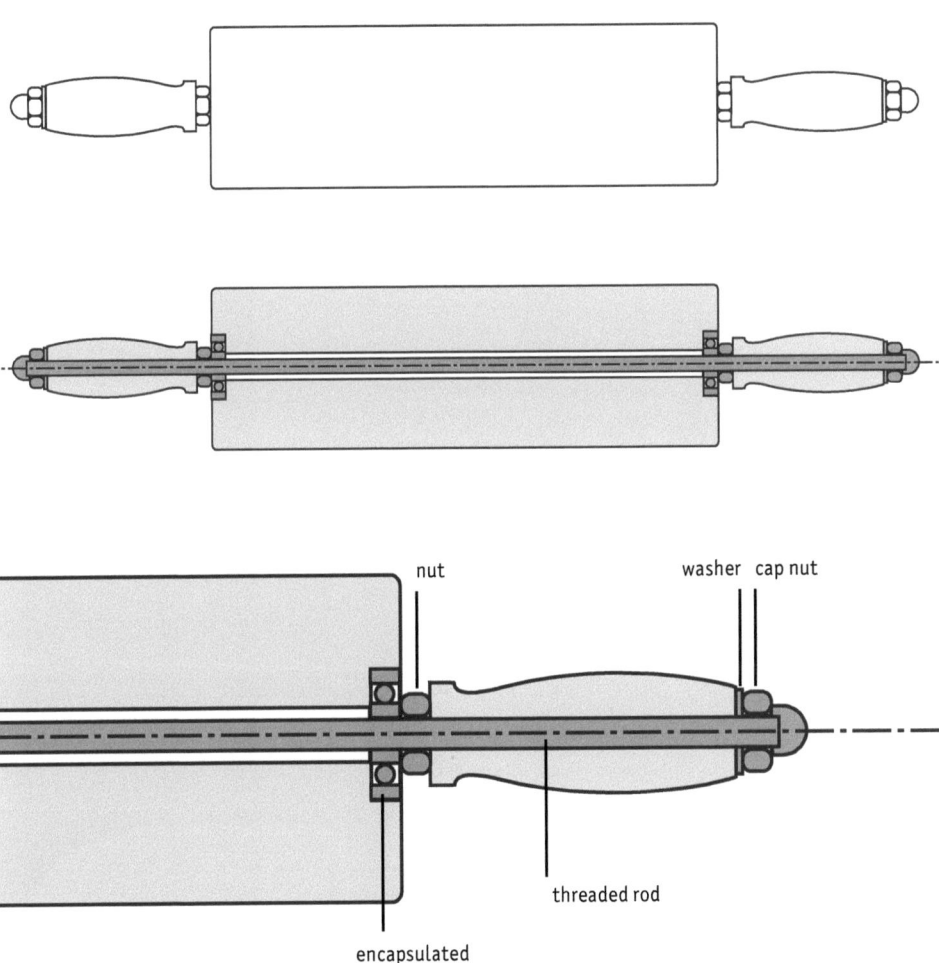

nut

washer cap nut

threaded rod

encapsulated
ball bearings

Shovel

A shovel can be made not only with the carving knife. It can also be made entirely on the lathe. Fruit trees are particularly suitable for turning such a utensil into a piece of art.

Procedure:

1 A scantling is scrubbed round between the centers. Both ends are cleaned at right angles.
2 Turning a suitable recess.
3 The workpiece is hollowed out from the front in the desired shape.
4 A wooden disc is turned to the right diameter as an auxiliary chuck.
5 The workpiece is clamped between the centres and made to have a uniform wall thickness on the outside. The handle is turned.
6 The excess material is sawn off with the band saw and sanded to a neat rounded shape.

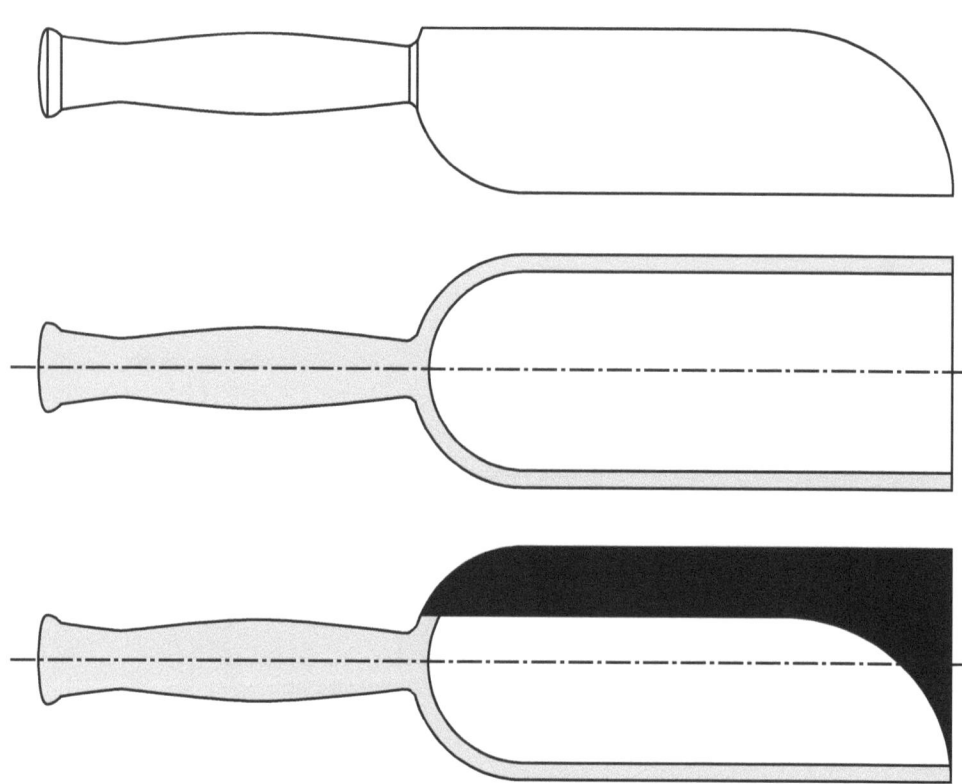

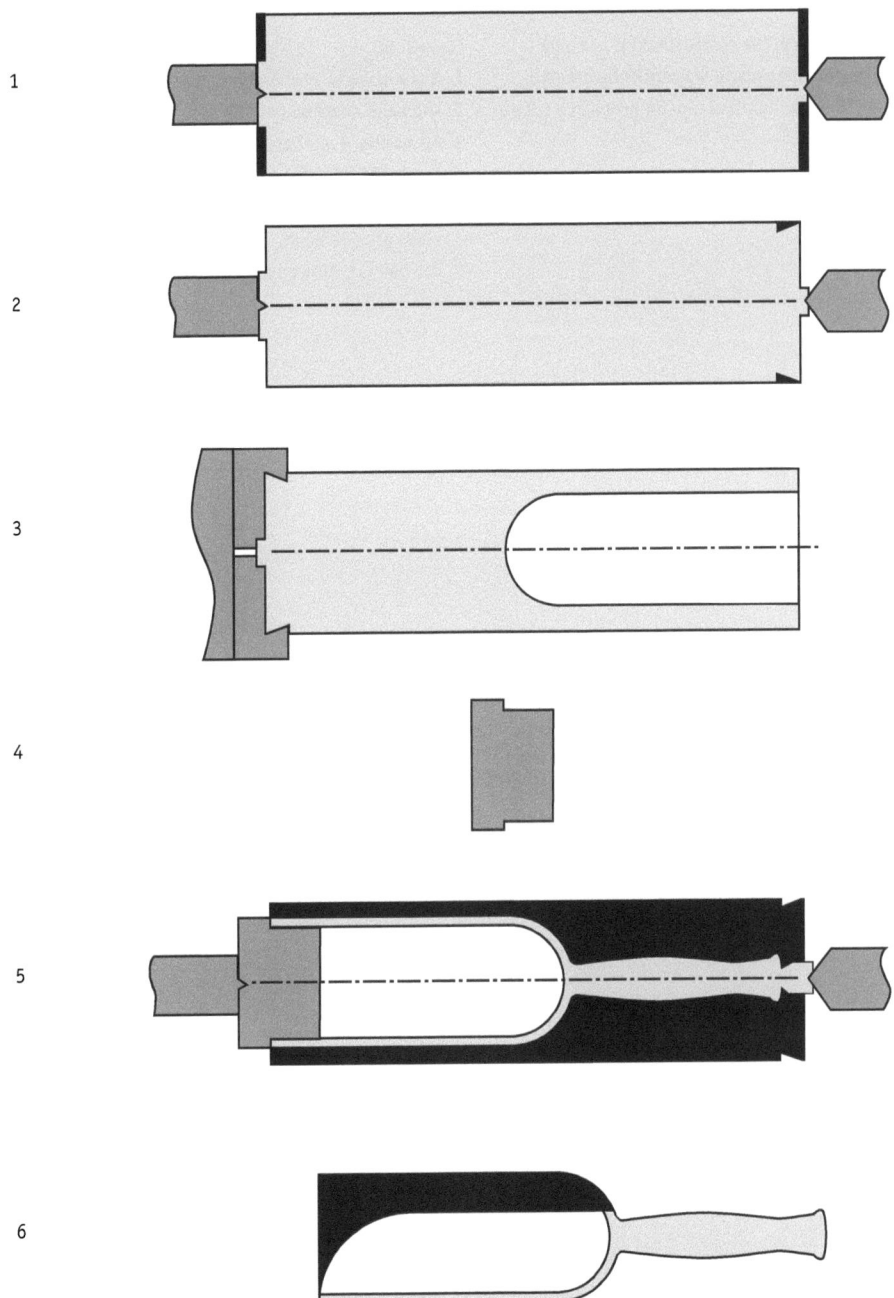

1

2

3

4

5

6

Coffee spoon

Made from one piece, the coffee spoon is not only a useful utensil. When made of beautifully grained wood, it is the most dignified tool for preparing coffee.

Procedure:

1 A scantling is scrubbed round between the centers.
2 The handle and ball are turned.
3 An auxiliary wooden chuck is made. A cutout is sawn for the handle of the spoon.
4 The workpiece is clamped. Slight moistening provides good tension.
5 The ball is hollowed out and the rim is shaped.

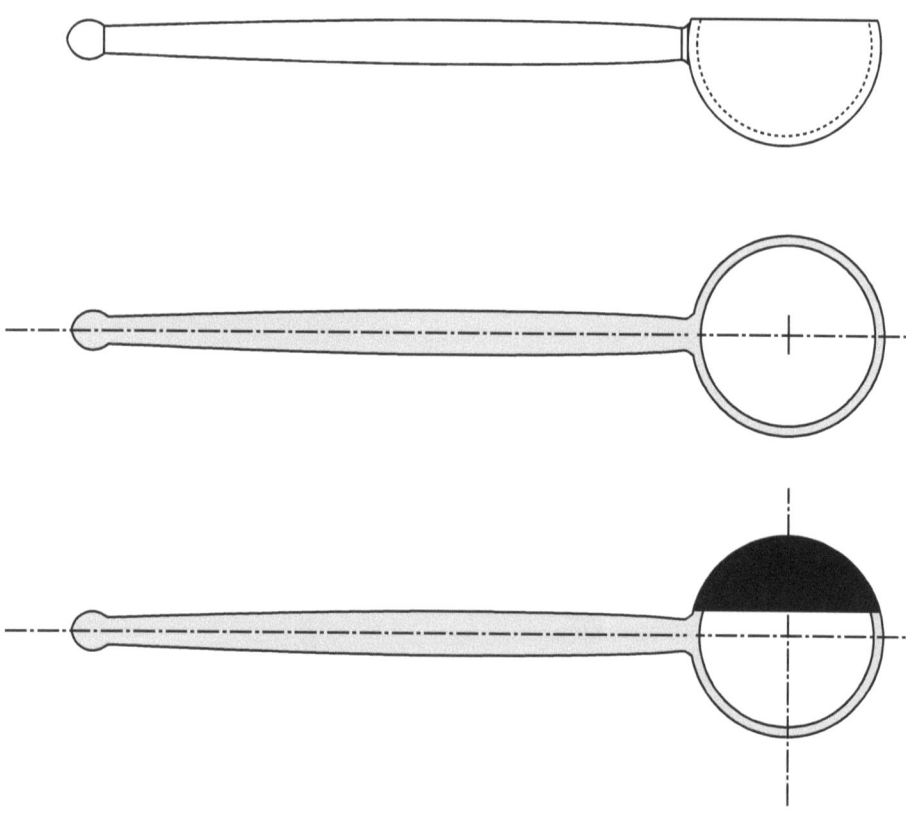

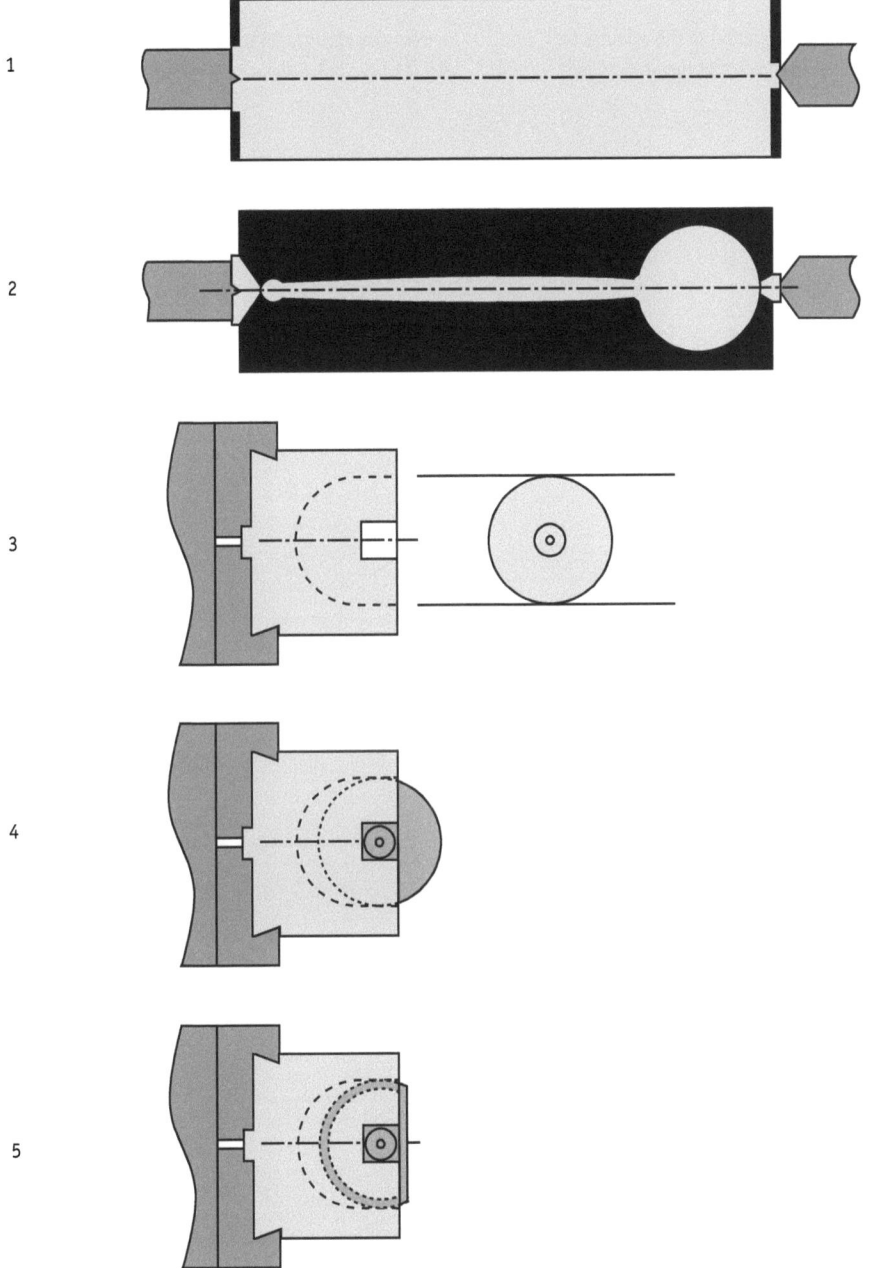

Bowl

Bowls have always been part of the woodturners' work. Recently, modern tong chucks have made bowl turning an everyday activity for woodturner enthusiasts as well. The examples show common shapes.

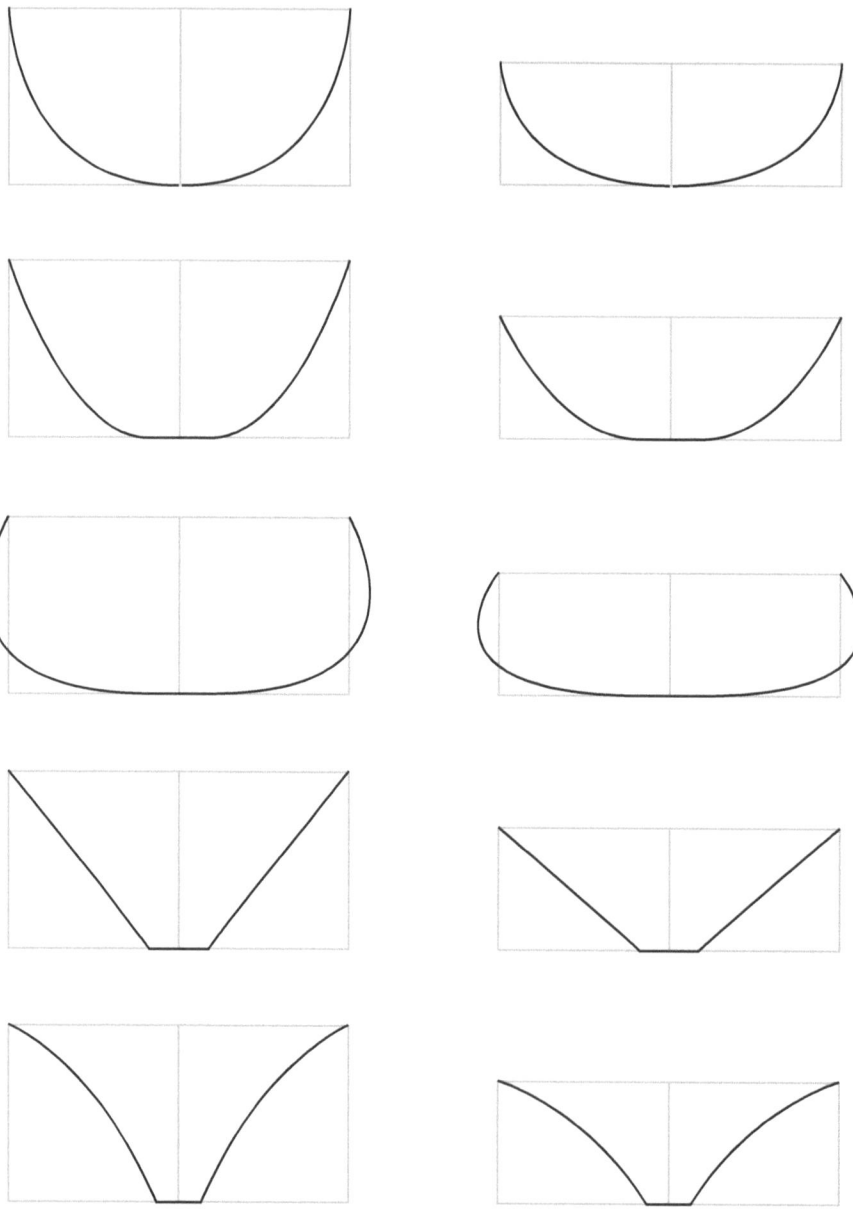

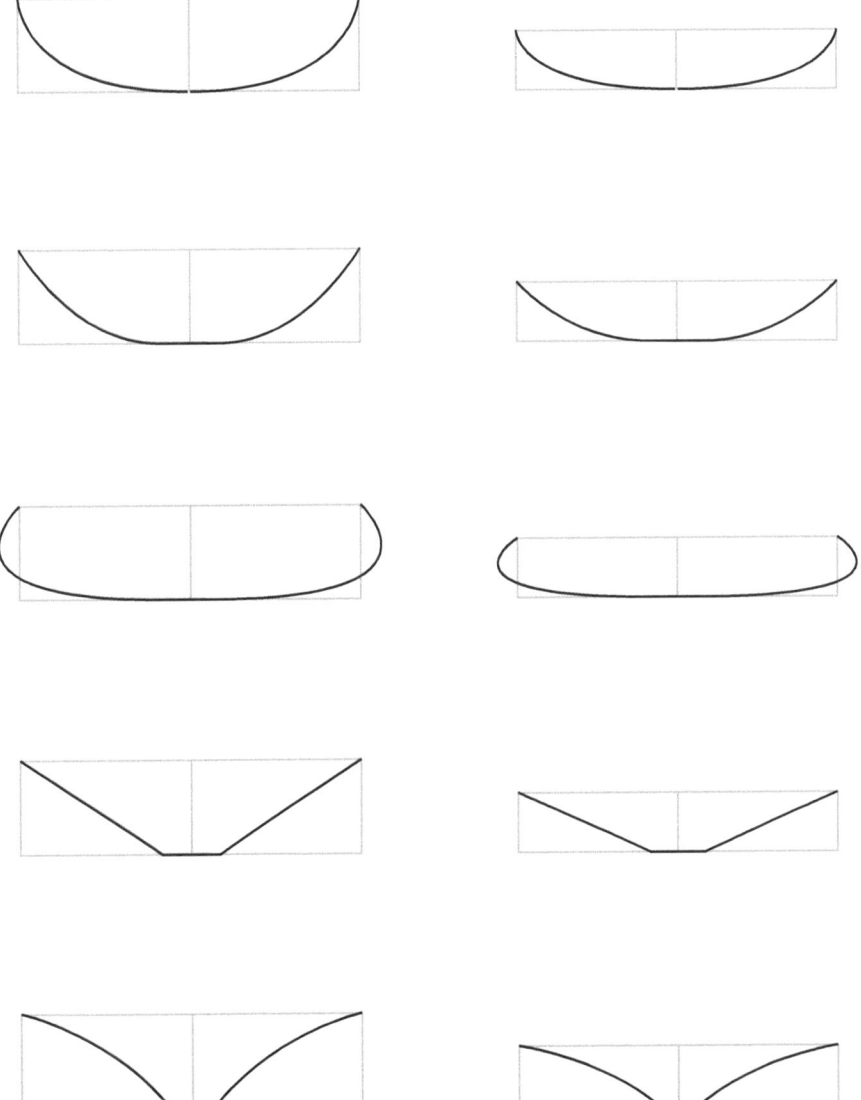

Vase

The bowls curves serve as a starting point for the
design of vases.

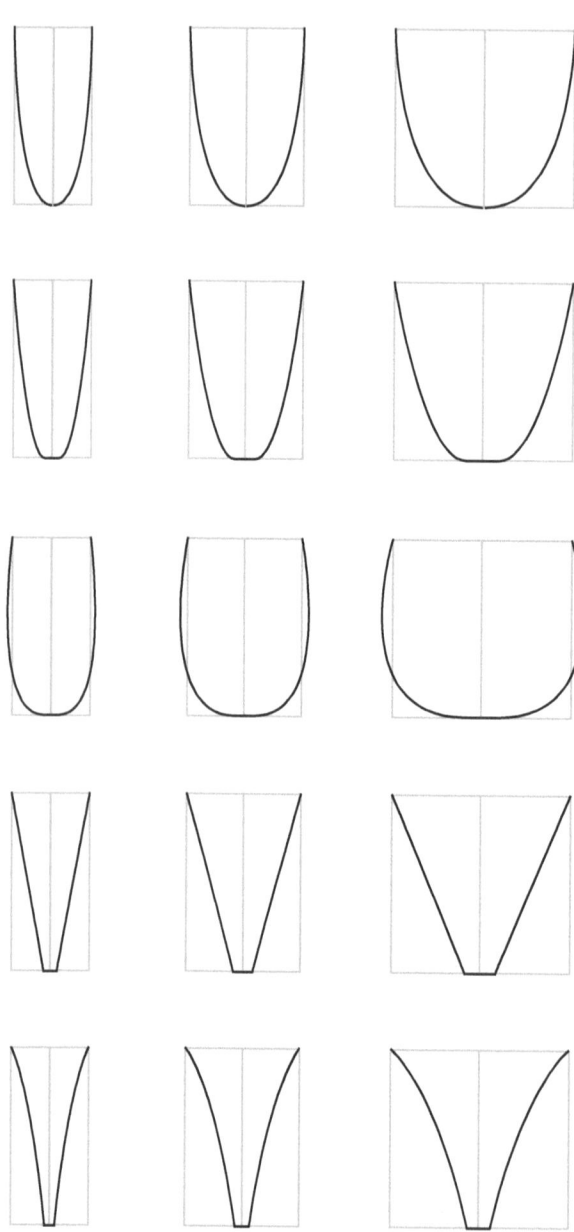

By adding a second curve, a multitude of new shapes emerge. Here the design changes only by shifting the height of the apex of the curve.

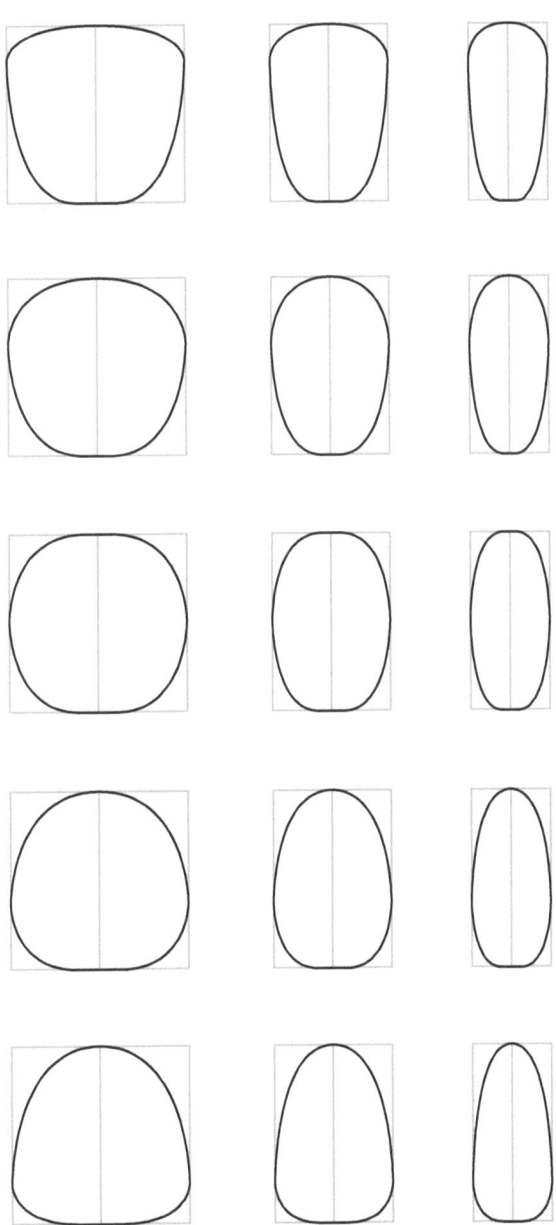

By adding a third line, the vase gets a neck or collar.
Here, too, the shape changes by shifting the apex.

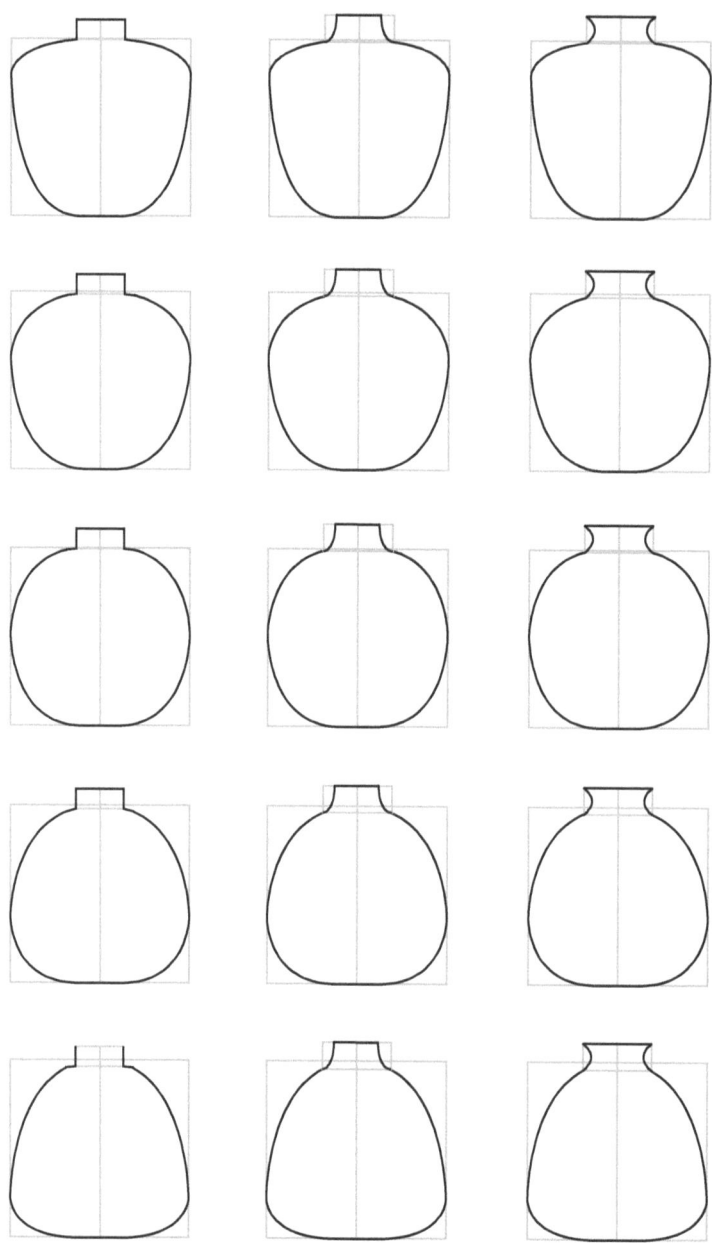

Here the shapes from the left side have again been changed in dimensions. This way it becomes possible to try endless possibilities until the ideal shape is found.

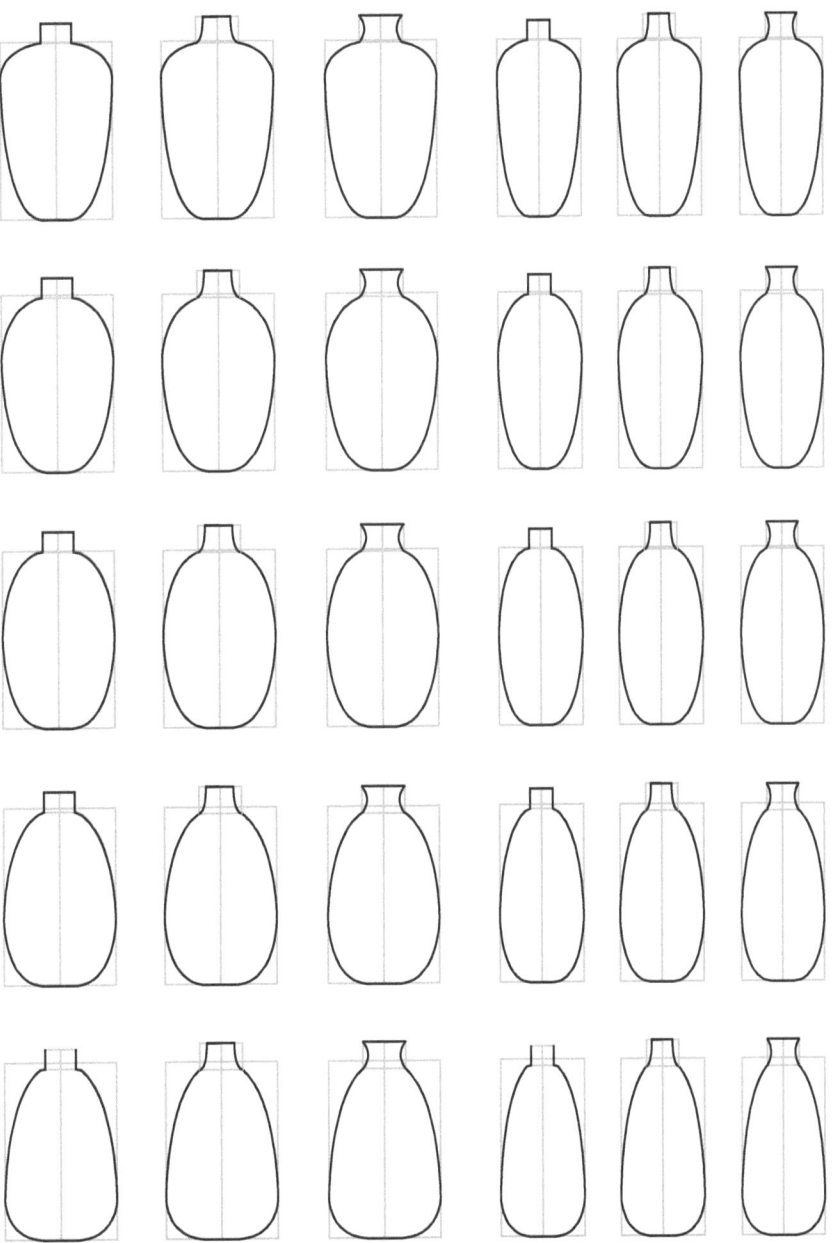

Caddies / Boxes

Caddies are available in many variations. Sizes and dimensions are adapted to the respective application. The fit of the lid also varies depending on the requirement. For example, Japanese tea caddies have two lids to protect the aroma. For jewellery boxes, one will choose a different design.

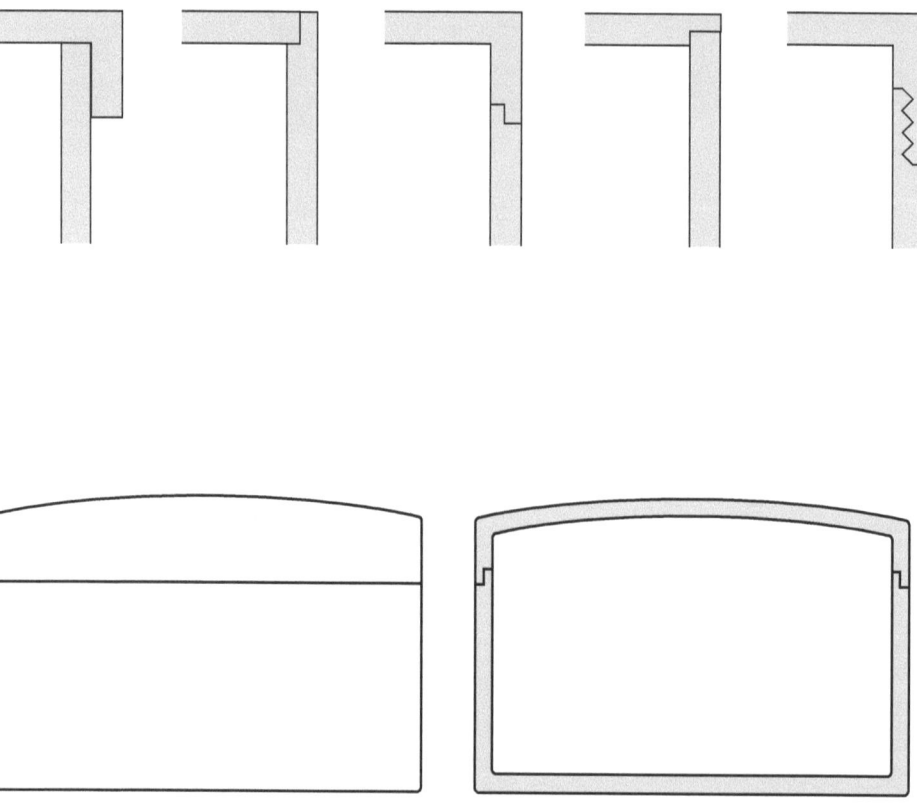

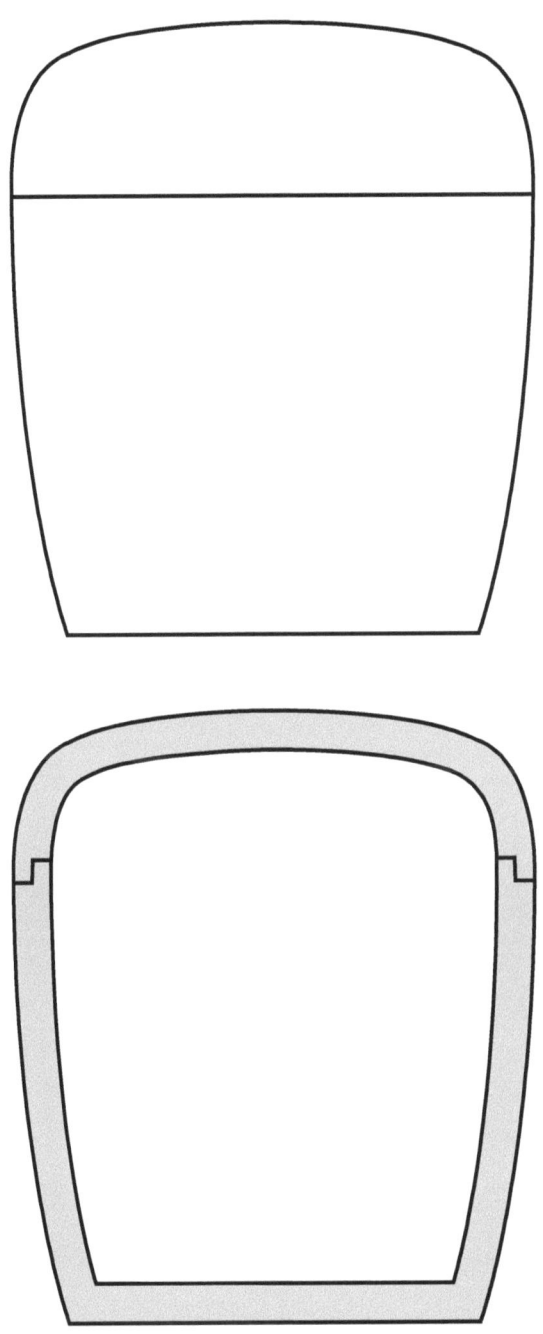

Japanese tea caddy

Old Japanese tea caddies are equipped with two lids to protect the aroma of the tea.

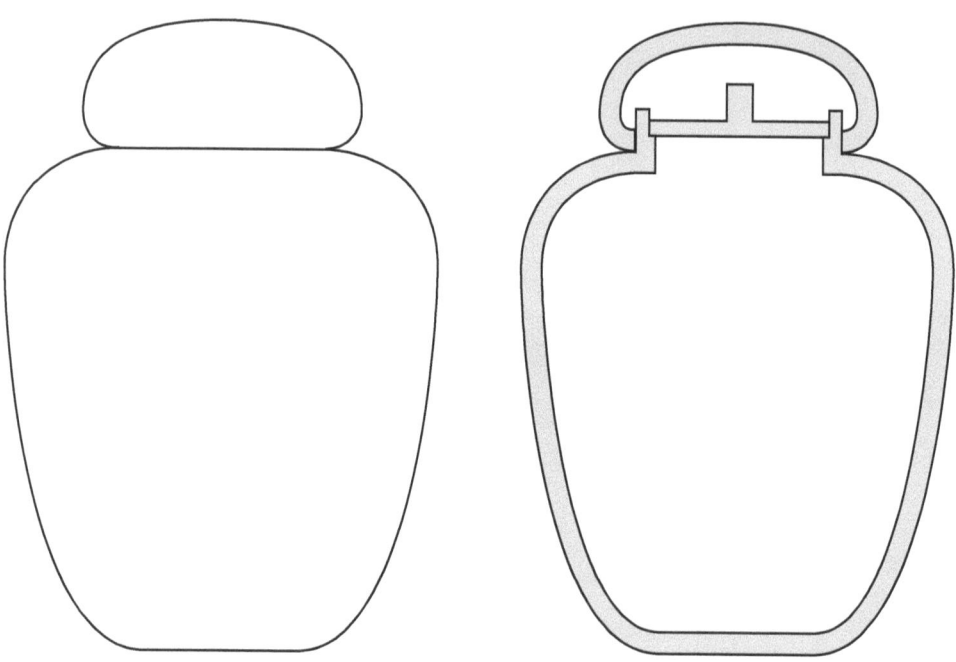

Cigar case

It doesn't get much more stylish than this: a cigar case
made of high-quality wood. One as plug-in version,
the other with a winding thread. The hole is drilled
with a drill of desired thickness.

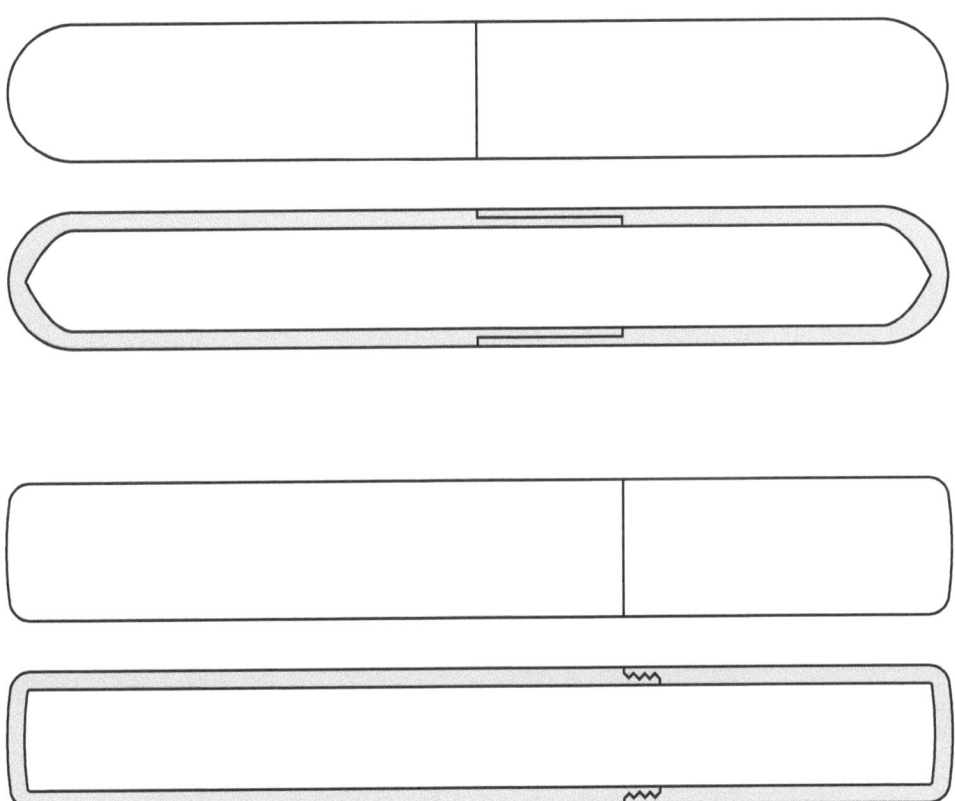